WORLD FILM LOCATIONS TORONTO

Edited by Tom Ue

First Published in the UK in 2014 by Intellect Books, The Mill, Parnall Road, Fishponds, Bristol, BS16 3JG, UK

First Published in the USA in 2014 by Intellect Books, The University of Chicago Press, 1427 E. 60th Street, Chicago, IL 60637, USA

Copyright ©2014 Intellect Ltd

Cover photo: *Cosmopolis* (2012) Alfama Films/Prospero Pictures/Kinology/ The Kobal Collection

Copy Editor: Emma Rhys

Typesetting: Jo Amner

A Catalogue record for this book is available from the British Library

World Film Locations Series
ISSN: 2045-9009
eISSN: 2045-9017

World Film Locations Toronto
ISBN:978-1-78320-195-2
ePDF ISBN: 978-1-78320-287-4
ePub ISBN: 978-1-78320-288-1

Printed and bound by Bell & Bain Limited, Glasgow

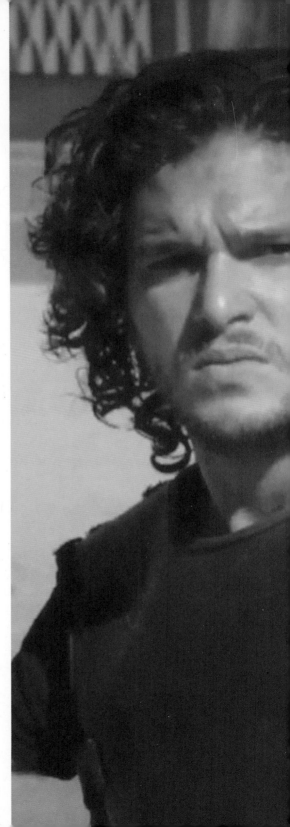

WORLD FILM LOCATIONS
TORONTO

EDITOR
Tom Ue

SERIES EDITOR & DESIGN
Gabriel Solomons

CONTRIBUTORS
Corey Waite Arnold
Noel Brown
Sheri Chriqui
Michael Da Silva
Richard Dennis
Lai-Tze Fan
David Fleischer
Steve Gravestock
Piers Handling
John James
Fiona Luck
Georgia Rushing Macey
Robert McGill
Tyler Shores
Will Straw
Carl Wilson

LOCATION PHOTOGRAPHY
Sheri Chriqui
Lai-Tze Fan
Kevin Harrison
Fiona Luck
Robert McGill
Will Straw
Tom Ue
Ontario Media Development Corporation

LOCATION MAPS
Jo Amner

PUBLISHED BY
Intellect
The Mill, Parnall Road,
Fishponds, Bristol, BS16 3JG, UK
T: +44 (0) 117 9589910
F: +44 (0) 117 9589911
E: *info@intellectbooks.com*

Bookends: *Enemy* (Rhombus Media/ Roxbury Pictures)
This page: *Pompeii* (Constantin Film Produktion)
Overleaf: *The F Word* (No Trace Camping/Caramel Film)

CONTENTS

ACKNOWLEDGEMENTS

My first and deepest debt is to my doctoral supervisor Philip Horne. I have been immensely fortunate to have Professor Horne as mentor, critic and example as teacher and writer; and I dedicate this book, my first, to him. I have benefited immeasurably from the intellectual and practical support of students, teachers and researchers, past and present, in the Department of English Language and Literature at University College London, and from the help of its administrative team, Carol Bowen, Stephen Cadywold, Anita Garfoot and James Phillips. Philip Schofield from the Faculty of Laws welcomed me warmly into the University College London Bentham Project, and I thank my colleagues there for their generosity and camaraderie.

David Fleischer has been an invaluable resource and his knowledge of Toronto on film is a constant inspiration. Kevin Harrison's location photography in many of the pages that follow brought the city to life. I have learned a lot from all of the book's contributors, especially Steve Gravestock, Fiona Luck and Tyler Shores, who made the editing process a pleasure. Noel Brown, Professor Horne, Robert McGill and Gravestock were tremendous influences on the book's introductory material. Over many years, the Toronto International Film Festival has nurtured me to be a much better film scholar, and I am grateful to Lina Rodriguez for her unflagging support. I have profited from the kindness of the many institutions represented in this book, and from Marsha Herle and Anna Shipside at the Ontario Media Development Corporation.

My particular thanks go to Gabriel Solomons, an exemplary designer, reader, colleague and friend, for inviting me to edit this project, for his unnerving perspicacity, and for his meticulousness; to Emma Rhys for her copyediting; and to Intellect and the University of Chicago Press for their scholarly care. For their encouragement and their votes of confidence, I am indebted to the Canadian Centennial Scholarship Fund; the Social Science and Humanities Research Council of Canada; and University College London.

TOM UE

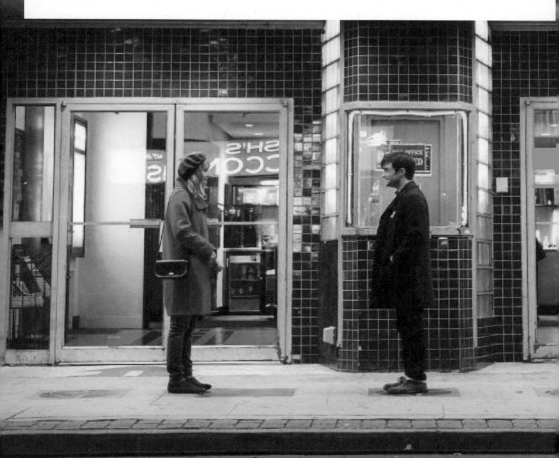

INTRODUCTION

World Film Locations *Toronto*

ERIC PACKER (ROBERT PATTINSON) reveals to his wife Elise (Sarah Gadon) in David Cronenberg's *Cosmopolis* (2012) that the cork lining that he had built into his stretch limousine failed to shut out the street noise:

The city eats and sleeps noise. It makes noise out of every century. It makes the same noise as it made in the seventeenth century, along with all the other noises that have evolved since then. No. I don't mind the noise. The noise energizes me. The important thing is that it's there.

The sounds that Cronenberg, through Packer, describes here gesture towards the historicity and the vitality of the city, a site of convergence between the past and the present, and of negotiation between distance and proximity, between estrangement and intimacy.

The rise and the proliferation of modern cities, which coincided with developments in photography and film, the symbiotic relationship between these two dynamics, and the issues in identity and representation that they provoke, form the strategic core of the *World Film Locations* books' collective thinking. This series explores the cultural relevance and the allure of cities for film-makers and audiences by contextualizing and by analysing how the medium has framed and informed our perception of the wider world.

This volume traces Toronto's historical progression into an international city; demonstrates the narrative interests that it has inspired amongst film-makers, both Canadian and international; and celebrates the city's 180th anniversary. It brings together over forty reviews of scenes from different films, each of which is accompanied by images of the scene, and, where possible, of the location today. The films represented here encompass a wide range of genres and periods – from family classics like Bob Clark's *A Christmas Story* (1983) to musicals like Adam Shankman's *Hairspray* (2007) – and of film-makers, from Don Owen (*Nobody Waved Good-bye* [1964]) to Edgar Wright (*Scott Pilgrim vs. the World* [2010]).

Alongside reviews, this book features 'spotlight' essays that explore the rise of films made in Toronto in the 1960s; the Yonge Street Strip and the Distillery District, at different periods, as two of the city's central movie locations; some of the masterpieces of the Toronto New Wave film-makers and their links to the theatre scene; domestic spaces in films; Cronenberg's use of Toronto, a city with which he is powerfully bonded; the rise of superhero films made in the city and its own hero in the character Kick-Ass; and the Toronto International Film Festival. As a whole, these essays, along with the reviews, provide us with both a framework for thinking about the city and an opportunity to look back and to look forward on Toronto's 180th anniversary. And if we listen, we too can hear, share and join in the symphony of voices that have stirred the imaginations of Guillermo del Toro, Atom Egoyan, Roland Joffé and Sarah Polley. ✢

Tom Ue, Editor

TORONTO

City of the Imagination

Text by
TOM
UE

WALLACE (DANIEL RADCLIFFE) sits on the roof of his three-storied apartment, looking from the sloping hills of Riverdale to downtown Toronto, lost in thought about the girl (Zoe Kazan) that he has met at a party earlier that night. He studies the slip of paper with the scrawled-on phone number that she gave him before he lets go of the page and a breeze carries it far away. For Linda Hutcheon, Canada speaks a doubled voice, something that incorporates irony, though not necessarily in a defensive or offensive way (1991, p. 1). Rather, it enables 'speakers to address and at the same time slyly confront an "official" discourse: that is, to work *within* a dominant tradition but also to challenge it – without being utterly co-opted by it' (1991, p. 1–2). Nowhere is this more evident than in the films made in Canada, and especially Toronto with its cosmopolitan and international make-up. Michael Dowse's and writer Elan Mastai's *The F Word* (2013), as we have seen, harkens back to the American rom-com – Wallace and Chantry are subsequently brought together by chance in a screening of *The*

Princess Bride (Rob Reiner, 1987) at the Royal no less – while situating the city in the genre's rich and vibrant history. Torontonians will resonate strongly with the film's 'geographical integrity', that is, its filmic locations' close approximation to where they are based in the real world.

Toronto's standing in for another city, though it is itself a modern one with its identity emerging in its own right, is part of its rather paradoxical presence in the global imagination. While the earliest recorded film footage that we have of Toronto is from George Scott's 1904 *The Great Toronto Fire, April 19, 1904*, which shows part of the massive blaze that destroyed 122 buildings, the city's cinematic self-image was not firmly established until the 1960s, with the emergence of Don Owen's, David Secter's, David Cronenberg's and Don Shebib's work (Handling, p. 15). Owen's *Nobody Waved Good-bye* (1964) captures the vulnerability and the frustrations of Peter (Peter Kastner) and Julie (Julie Biggs), 18-year-olds who aim not to emulate their constantly fighting parents. In a pivotal moment in the film, Peter reprimands his future brother-in-law, a dentist, for his capitalist values, and for his going to see Joseph L. Mankiewicz's highly-publicized *Cleopatra* (1963), with its star Elizabeth Taylor. Peter's desire to define himself against the dentist finds correlation in the film's desire to define itself against the more commercial American feature, and this is apparent in the stark realism of Owen's film. For all Peter's idealism, he is unable to escape the capitalist culture that he criticizes. The film repeatedly uses, as a visual cue, roads and the subway – Peter and Julie take the train from the Rosedale to the Davisville Stations in the early hours – to remind us that the characters are in transition, both physically and emotionally.

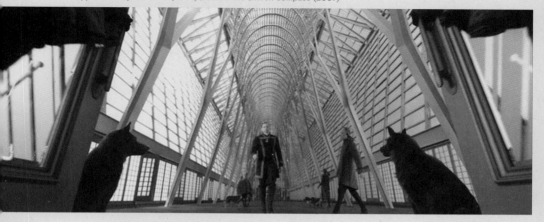

Above ©2007 New Line Cinema/Ingenious Film Partners
Opposite © 2006 Foundry Films; Capri Releasing; HanWay Films

The city's film scene in the past thirty years changed, importantly, with the rise of Canadian cinema, the founding of the Montreal World Film Festival in 1975 and the Toronto International Film Festival (known originally as 'The Festival of Festivals') in 1976, events that have the potential 'to help shape and confirm as well as contest the canon' (Czach, pp. 78–80). Toronto has inspired the imaginations of numerous film-makers since. Its representation as Boston in Good Will Hunting (Gus van Sant, 1997), the titular city in Chicago (Rob Marshall, 2002), Lyra's world in The Golden Compass (Chris Weitz, 2007), New York in Cosmopolis (David Cronenberg, 2012), and the ancient city of Pompeii (Paul W.S. Anderson, 2014) are just some of numerous instances in which the city is disguised as somewhere else. Indeed, a cursory glance at filming statistics would indicate the sheer number and range of film projects at home in the city and the number of masks that it wears: in 2012, expenditures for on-location filming in Toronto reached an approximate $1.2 billion; for major productions (inclusive of features, television specials, series and movies of the week), $1.0149 billion; for 103 television series with a combined 1,009 episodes, $707.33 million; and for 40 features, $278.1 million ('Film, Television, Commercial and Music Video Production'). The

dual identities of the city as both itself and, more often, as another place contribute to the informed viewer's experience a far-ranging kind of irony by imbuing it with multiple ways of reading.

In Sarah Polley's *Away from Her* (2006), Fiona's doctor (Alberta Watson) asks her (Julie Christie) what she would do if she were the first person to spot a fire in a movie theatre. Fiona, who is suffering from Alzheimer's disease, replies, as she looks to her husband Grant (Gordon Pinsent) for confirmation, 'We don't go to the movies much anymore, do we, Grant? All those multiplexes showing the same American garbage'. This nod to American cinema, its monotony, and its global distribution recalls Peter's in Don Owen's film and reminds us of how much the city and its film culture have changed since. This criticism prompts us to reflect on the film's own beginnings as a short story by Nobel Prize winner Alice Munro that was set in Brant County, Ontario and that was first published in *The New Yorker*; its premiere in the Toronto International Film Festival; and its global recognition through numerous accolades including Academy Award nominations for Polley and Christie. The questions that *Away from Her* and numerous other films raise about irony speak to the doubleness that Hutcheon describes. These metanarrative elements make Toronto and its representations on screens large and small a particularly illuminating space for the imagination. ✠

NOTE: See Robert McGill's 'No Nation but Adaptation: "The Bear Came over the Mountain," *Away from Her*, and What It Means to Be Faithful' (2008) for an insightful discussion about the film and how it 'speaks to the significance of adaptation for a country in which many artists and critics have been preoccupied with building a sense of national cultural heritage' (p. 110).

Toronto's standing in for another city, though it is itself a modern one with its identity emerging in its own right, is part of its rather paradoxical presence in the global imagination.

RAW YOUTH

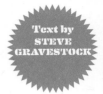

Text by
STEVE
GRAVESTOCK

ALTHOUGH A HANDFUL of features were made in Toronto before 1960, most of them were barely, if at all, released. Toronto-based film-makers like Norman Jewison and Ted Kotcheff began their careers working for Canadian television, the only place to learn their craft at the time, and eventually left for Hollywood and London. Others, like Sidney J. Furie and Julian Roffman, made independent features but soon decided that English Canada lacked the infrastructure to support film-makers, and they decamped as well. English Canadian and Toronto-based cinema was essentially born in the 1960s with a series of films focusing on young people.

One of the first serious English Canadian feature films to be set in Toronto, and to break through and reach a domestic audience, Don Owen's *Nobody Waved Good-bye* (1964), was initially intended to be a National Film Board (NFB)-funded short docudrama about middle-class juvenile delinquents. But, according to legend, Owen shot the film in the summer when

his superiors at the NFB were on vacation. He simply kept ordering more film stock and returned to Montreal with a feature-length fiction work. (The NFB, of course, specialized exclusively in documentary.) The film would have been buried and forgotten had it not been successful at the New York Film Festival, which spurred its domestic re-release. Much of the film was improvised and shot on location using 16 mm equipment, which afforded the film-makers an unusual amount of freedom and imbued the film with a documentary aura – so much so that it won the BAFTA for Best Documentary.

Owen drew on his own experiences of the city, to some extent, and especially on the personality of actor Peter Kastner in creating his hero, Peter, an antsy adolescent and nascent artist who almost naturally rubs people the wrong way, but whose problems and concerns are either ignored or dismissed in the most peremptory manner. His elders are so intent on rules and regulations that they seem determined to ruin Peter's life. One of the key players in the film is Toronto, then a sadly mono-cultural city, and stodgy to the extreme. (The hyper-stuffiness of the milieu only makes the hero more sympathetic.)

Owen once referred to the Toronto of the period – where bars, cinemas and restaurants closed on Sundays – as 'Laura Secord' heaven, referencing the long running chain of sweets stores named after an early national heroine. Key scenes take place on Toronto Island; on Highway 401; and in pre-hippie Yorkville, where coffee shops were just on the verge of exploding. A couple of years later, Yorkville will become the stomping grounds for Neil Young, Joni Mitchell, Gordon Lightfoot and, briefly, Rick James.

Another key early film was David Secter's *Winter Kept Us Warm* (1965). Set primarily on the University of Toronto campus, it deals with

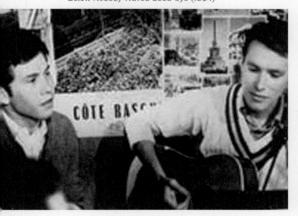

Above © 1964 National Film Board of Canada (NFB)
Opposite © 1965 Varsity

the friendship between Doug (John Labow), a sophisticated returning student, and Peter (Henry Tarvainen), a naïve freshman from the provinces. Secter cross-cuts between the two characters' arrivals with Doug speeding down the highway in a convertible blasting bebop while Peter emerges from Union Station to stare in wonder at the statuesque Royal York Hotel – now the Fairmount Royal York. Doug takes Peter under his wing and helps him acclimate to big city life, but their friendship hits a snag when Peter takes up with a young girl (Janet Amos) and Doug becomes increasingly jealous and ostracized. Deeply courageous and heartfelt, *Winter* was one of the first films to deal openly with homosexuality and it was one of the first Canadian films to be invited to the Cannes International Film Festival. Stylistically, it suggests a lower budget *Shadows* (John Casavettes, 1959) with a few amateurish flourishes (see the still photo montage of campus life near the beginning) resulting from the film-maker's attempt to do too much with a tiny budget, most of which was provided by the student council. Boasting almost bucolic footage of the University of Toronto campus (some locations remain largely unchanged), the film famously inspired David Cronenberg, then a science major, to make movies. Paul Hoffert composed the score.

> **Deeply courageous and heartfelt, *Winter* was one of the first films to deal openly with homosexuality and it was one of the first Canadian films to be invited to the Cannes International Film Festival.**

Secter's second film, *The Offering* (1967), was not as well-received, though it dealt with a subject as groundbreaking – an interracial romance between a young dancer from China and a white stagehand at the beloved concert venue Massey Hall. Unlike his fellow filmmakers, Secter seemed genuinely impressed with Toronto, especially its increasingly modern, futuristic look. A tracking shot climbing the front of the recently built City Hall is full of optimism, wonder and even awe.

Clarke Mackey's *The Only Thing You Know* (1971) picks up where *Nobody* left off, focusing on confused, disenchanted, middle-class youth. Like Don Owen's Peter, high school senior Ann (Ann Knox) is uncertain about and confused by the world around her, and she receives little or no help from her parents who are constantly exasperated by her and openly anxious for her to leave the nest. (If anything, Ann's parents are even meaner than Peter's — berating her within earshot.) In the intervening years between the films, though, the post-World War II/baby boomer generation in North America had been politicized by the second wave of feminism, the sexual revolution and the war in Vietnam, among other things – and these developments figure prominently in the movie. The opening scene, for instance, records a protest against the American presence in Vietnam and Ann's best friend, Laura (Linda Hoffman) complains volubly about the other women in her feminist discussion group. (They prefer to talk about picayune subjects like their boyfriends.)

Ann's conflicts and disappointments are not restricted to the older generation. Laura betrays her; her boyfriend Scott (Allan Royal), a teacher, does not understand her adolescent melancholia and uncertainty; and Scott's hippie draft dodger friend, Paul (John Denos), seduces and abandons her. For all that, the central opposition does not centre on political views but instead contrasts the articulate (and therefore suspect) with the uncertain and confused as in *Nobody*, the film that inspired the 14-year-old Mackey to become a director. *The Only Thing You Know* is set specifically in Toronto with a key scene taking place in the business district where hippie Paul is infuriated and imperiled by the midday rush. The film's version of heavy traffic seems oddly quaint given how much larger and more densely populated the city is today. On the other hand, the fabled blues bar Grossman's Tavern, once the watering hole for 1960s folkies and a regular hangout for blues guitarist Jeff Healey – and where Scott first picks up Ann – seems peculiarly unchanged. ✚

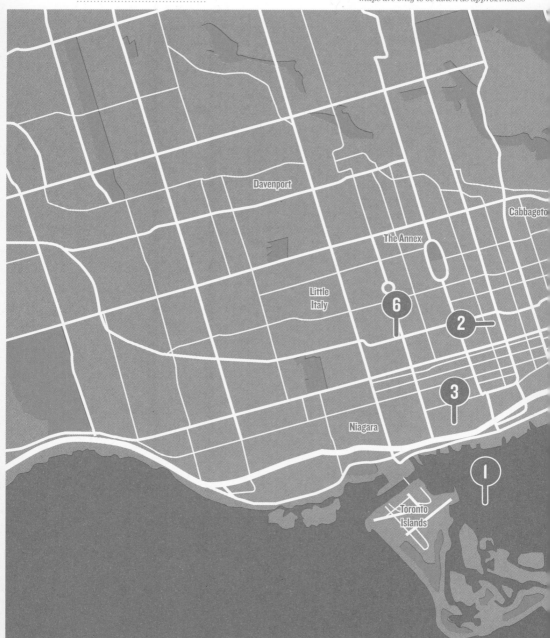

TORONTO LOCATIONS
SCENES 1-6

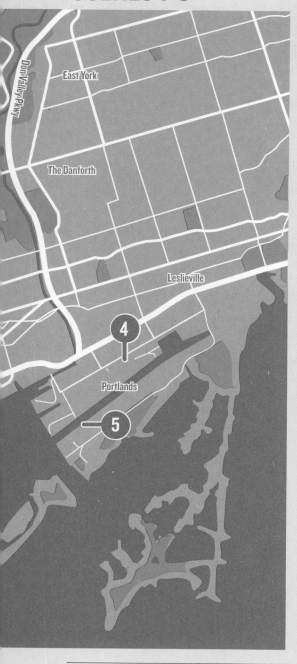

PADDLE TO THE SEA (1966)

LOCATION *Toronto Inner Harbour*

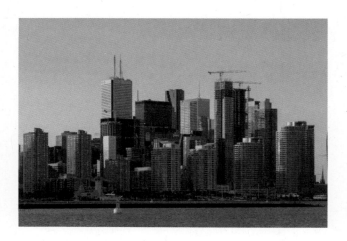

TORONTO'S APPEARANCE in Bill Mason's classic short is brief and unnerving. The NFB film's hero is a wood-carved Aboriginal figurine named Paddle to the Sea who sits in a miniature canoe, floating from Northern Ontario to the Atlantic through the Great Lakes and the St Lawrence Seaway. After he plunges over Niagara Falls, we are told 'he disappeared'. Cue a 14-second tracking shot that follows the little canoeist at night as he crosses the Toronto harbour with the skyline behind him. Nothing is said. Neither people nor other boats appear. The buildings are grainy outlines topped by neon signs. Is this Canada's version of Hell? of Limbo? The sight of an Indigenous canoeist before a dark, electric city is sublime and haunting. One might recall that Toronto was built on First Nations land, and that while the city now has one of the largest Aboriginal North American populations in the world, it has been represented by Aboriginal writers as alienating and dangerous, a place where far too many Indigenous people have disappeared in one way or another. If Mason's protagonist manages to reach the ocean, it is not least because Toronto fails to snare him. In the meantime, twenty-first-century viewers are unlikely to recognize the skyline the movie records. In 1966, there were no skyscrapers, no CN Tower, no waterfront high-rise condos. Toronto in *Paddle to the Sea* is uncanny, a lurking possibility, its cameo appearance suggesting a city that still awaits its speaking parts and star turns.
➽Robert McGill

Directed by Bill Mason
Scene description: 'Paddle' glides by the Toronto waterfront at night
Timecode for scene: 0:18:33 – 0:18:47

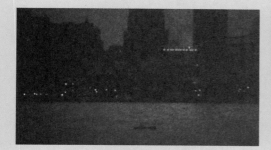 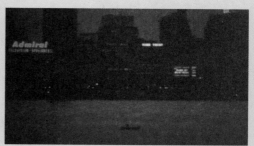

THE SILENT PARTNER (1978)

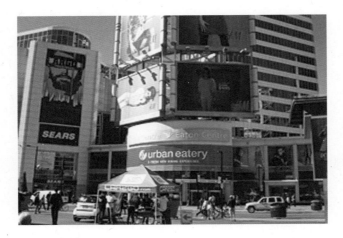

IN THE 1970S, Toronto began its ascent from a drab Protestant town into a modern world city. One sign of the new Toronto (for better or worse) was the reclamation of a long block of downtown Yonge Street as the 300-store Toronto Eaton Centre mall. Another was its eager embrace of B-grade Hollywood productions that came north to take advantage of lucrative tax breaks. The tax-shelter era produced virtually no films worth remembering but a rare exception is *The Silent Partner*, a smart, violent crime caper whose fate will forever be bound to that of its contemporary, the Eaton Centre. The story is a simple cat-and-mouse game between a psychopathic bank robber played by Christopher Plummer and the meek teller who tries to outsmart him at his own game, played by 1970s leading man de rigeur, Elliot Gould. Gould's bank is located in the mall's lower level and much of the action – including Plummer trying to get back his funds while dressed in drag – takes place there. Though it is easy to chuckle at the era's fashions and some of the mall's long-gone stores (e.g. The Orange Cup, The Slack Shack), the forward-looking, airy, white-and-glass design by local architect Eberhard Zeidler is captured in all its youthful glory. It would be a few more years until Hollywood North emerged in earnest, but *The Silent Partner* and Eaton Centre give a sense of the more cosmopolitan Toronto soon to come.

David Fleischer

Photo © Tom Ue

Directed by Daryl Duke
Scene description: Miles Cullen works at the Toronto Eaton Centre
Timecode for scene: 0:00:00 – 0:02:00

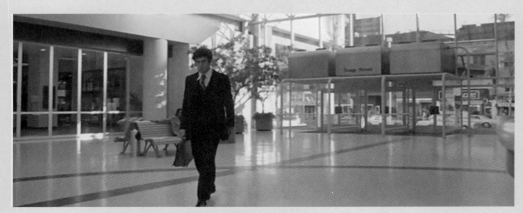

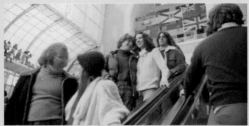

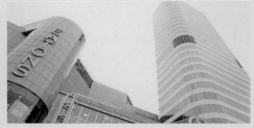

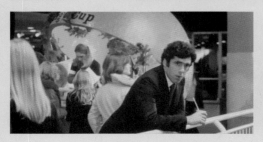

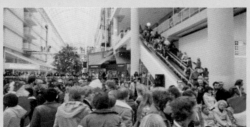

HIGHPOINT (1982)

LOCATION

CN Tower, 301 Front Street West

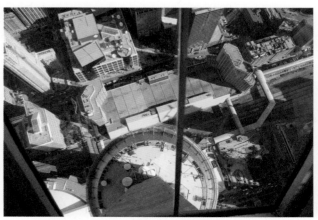

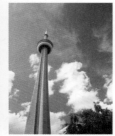

NO BOOK ON TORONTO would be complete without the CN Tower. Usually it ends up on the cutting-room floor so that Toronto can better resemble Boston or Chicago, or more often than not, New York. However, the CN Tower plays the starring role in *Highpoint*'s climactic scene. After swindling both the CIA and the Mafia out of millions, and framing unemployed accountant Lewis Kinney (Richard Harris) as a murderer, James Hatcher (Christopher Plummer) is on the run. A slapstick comedy of errors ensues culminating in a hair-raising finale set in Toronto's most recognizable landmark. With the heist gone wrong, Plummer plunges off the roof of – at the time – the world's tallest structure. Built by the Canadian National Railway Company for the practical purpose of getting better radio and television signals, the CN Tower demonstrated the growing strength of Canadian industry and sheer brilliance in engineering. Over the years it has added features such as a glass floor and the 'Edgewalk', where intrepid tourists can take an open-air tethered stroll 356 meters above the ground. It has furthered Toronto's journey into becoming a world-class city in terms of innovation and business investment, and provided it with an internationally recognized symbol. *Highpoint* itself was not as ubiquitous; surprisingly enough, a campy high-speed horse and buggy chase did not win it any Oscars. However, Toronto native Plummer and his stuntman Dar Robinson would agree that the heart-stopping fall at the end is worth a look. ⤖*Fiona Luck*

Photo © Kevin Harrison

Directed by Peter Carter
Scene description: Attempting a getaway with stolen millions,
James Hatcher plummets off the CN Tower
Timecode for scene: 1:20:56 – 1:22:37

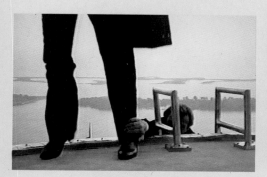 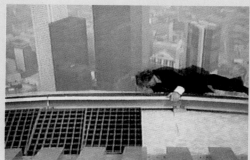

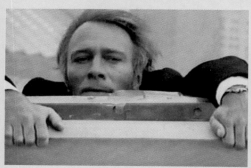 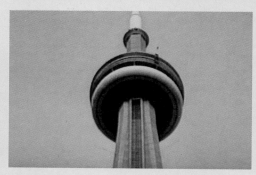

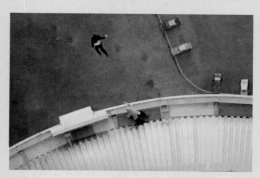 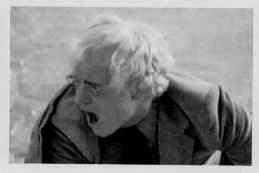

VIDEODROME (1983)

LOCATION *Stretch of dockland, Port Lands*

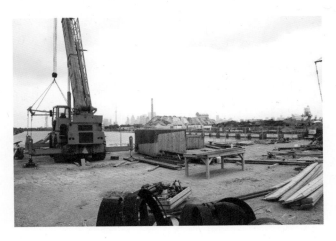

AS WITH MANY of Cronenberg's films, *Videodrome* – one of the director's most enigmatic productions – is not only filmed but fictionally located in his home city of Toronto (a fact which partly reflects the very limited budget on which the movie was produced). The film centres on Max Renn (James Woods), the owner of a small, disreputable cable-TV station who wishes to expand beyond his current reliance on soft-core pornography and discovers a pirate stream showing a snuff television series called 'Videodrome'. This, in reality, is merely a carrier for a mind-control signal developed by an extremist, underground political organization. Befitting its darkly paranoid themes and often-grotesque sequences of body horror, much of the outside location filming is purposely drab, with muted, grey colour tones and bewilderingly large, faceless (and comparatively anonymous) urban landscapes. Various tracking shots follow Renn's movements through the financial districts after he comes under Videodrome's pernicious influence, and begins a rapid descent into psychosis. Other scenes prominently display buildings in Queen Street East, Wellington Street (now part of Brookfield Place), Bathurst and Adelaide, and St Clair Avenue. The climax – in which a now-totally-psychotic Renn, having committed several murders, retreats to a condemned tugboat on the docklands – is filmed on a desolate-looking, abandoned stretch on the Port Lands. It is here that Renn, having been counter-programmed and under the belief that to eradicate Videodrome he must move beyond 'the old flesh', turns his gun on himself, bringing the film to an appropriately grim end.
❖ Noel Brown

Photo © Kevin Harrison

Directed by David Cronenberg
Scene description: Protagonist Max Renn retreats to an abandoned stretch of
docklands for the film's climactic scene and kills himself
Timecode for scene: 1:40:50 – 1:42:45

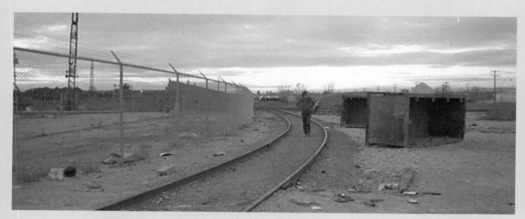

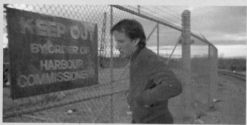

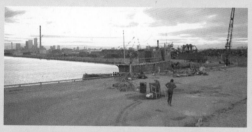

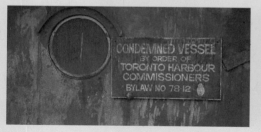

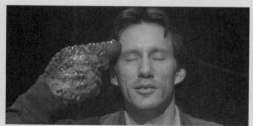

A CHRISTMAS STORY (1983)

LOCATION

Cherry Street, along the Cherry Street Bridge

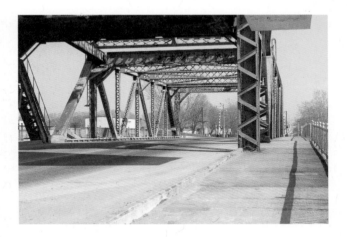

A CHRISTMAS STORY has become as much of a 25 December tradition as fireplace stockings, or (Chinese) turkey. Based on the stories of Jean Shepherd – who is the film's adult Ralphie narrator and who also makes a cameo appearance in the Higbee's department store – the film has endeared itself to audiences for being a story about childhood as much as it is about Christmas. Ralphie Parker (Peter Billingsley) really desires only one thing, 'the holy grail of Christmas gifts', in the form of 'a Red Ryder BB gun with a compass in the stock, and this thing which tells time'. When the family Oldsmobile gets a flat tire on the bridge in the memorable 'only I didn't say fudge' scene, his Old Man's (Darren McGavin) frenzied tire-changing causes a hubcap to be knocked out of Ralphie's hands, with bolts sent flying everywhere leading to the infamous expletive in slow motion, accompanied by the strains of Tchaikovsky's *Hamlet Overture* (1888). As punishment, Ralphie gets a bar of Life Buoy soap in the mouth for saying 'the queen-mother of dirty words, the F-dash-dash-dash word'. Set somewhere around the 1930s and 1940s in a Norman Rockwell-era nostalgic America, the story takes place in the fictional town of Hohman, Indiana. Various scenes of the film were shot in and around Toronto – Toronto's trademark Red Rocket trolleys are visible during scenes – with the 'fudge' scene shot at the southern end of Cherry Street in the industrial Port Lands district. Sharp-eyed viewers of the scene might also notice the Cherry Street Bridge in the background. Built in 1931, the officially named 'Cherry Street Strauss Trunnion Bascule Bridge' hinges open to allow the passage of tall ships, and it was recognized by the city as being architecturally historical. **Tyler Shores**

Photo © Ontario Media Development Corporation

Directed by Bob Clark
Scene description: Ralphie Parker tries to help his Old Man change a tire
on the family Oldsmobile, 'only he didn't say fudge'
Timecode for scene: 0:38:58 – 0:42:15

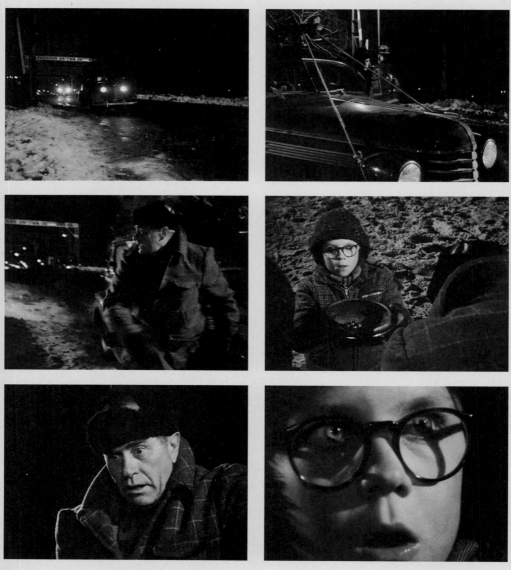

Images © 1983 Metro-Goldwyn-Meyer

POLICE ACADEMY (1984)

The Silver Dollar Room, 486 Spadina Avenue

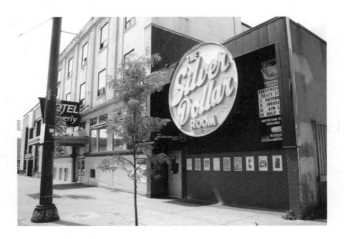

DEVOTED POLICE ACADEMY fans may not find the fictional Blue Oyster Bar on Howell Street, but for the next best thing, they might visit The Silver Dollar Room in downtown Toronto's Kensington Market neighbourhood. When Carey Mahoney (Steven Guttenberg) sends the unwitting Blankes (Brant von Hoffman) and Copeland (Scott Thomson) to the stereotypical gay leather biker bar, the ensuing all night dance marathon scenes – complete with disco ball and checkerboard dance floor – were filmed entirely within The Silver Dollar Room. The gag would end up being so popular that the Blue Oyster would make recurring appearances in three of the six *Police Academy* sequels. In addition, the peculiarly recognizable song in the scene (the 1974 tango called 'El Bimbo') would enjoy its own unique cult status thanks to the Blue Oyster Bar. Built in 1958 as a cocktail lounge for the nearby Hotel Waverly, The Silver Dollar Room continues to be one of Toronto's most popular nightclubs for blues and live music. Its no-frills atmosphere has retained much of the art deco look and feel from its earlier history, which endears the club to its regulars. Recently, development plans have proposed turning the existing nearby buildings into a twenty-story residential complex to serve as University of Toronto student housing. The Silver Dollar Room is expected to occupy the first floor of the new building, and continue its legacy as one of the city's most enduring music venues. ❖ *Tyler Shores*

Photo © Kevin Harrison

Directed by Hugh Wilson
Scene description: Blankes and Copeland unwittingly take part
in an all-night dance marathon at the Blue Oyster Bar
Timecode for scene: 0:44:06 – 0:44:38; 0:45:10 – 0:45:36

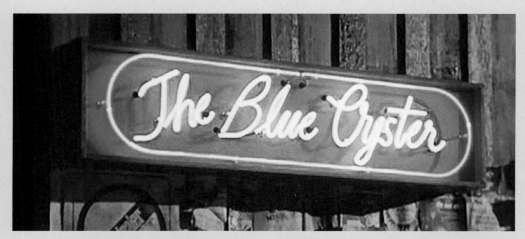

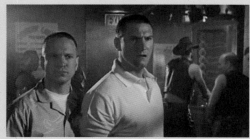

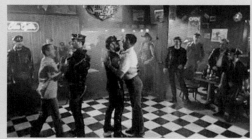

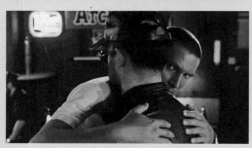

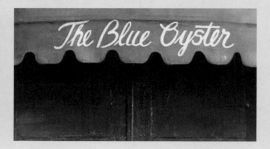

THE YONGE STREET STRIP

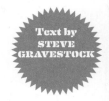

Text by
STEVE
GRAVESTOCK

THE TORONTO SHOWCASED in films in the 1960s may not have seemed the liveliest or most welcoming place, but the Toronto depicted in the 1970s was possibly even more inhospitable. The decade was ushered in with Don Shebib's iconic *Goin' Down the Road* (1970), about two Nova Scotia lads who head to the big city to escape a dire future, only to find that Toronto is far from friendly, even downright hostile. Their lives are split between their jobs and their grim flats, and their existences are brightened only by trips to Yonge Street and the record store A & A's – not the more iconic Sam the Record Man's as legend and other sources have it. (Their addiction to Yonge Street is mocked, to hilarious effect, in a *Second City* parody starring John Candy and Joe Flaherty.) Yet that film was practically upbeat compared to what followed.

Part of this negative mood was probably attributable to changes in how the Canadian Filmmaker Development Corporation (the CFDC, soon to be renamed Telefilm) funded projects. The momentum created by the critical and commercial successes of *Nobody Waved Good-bye* (Don Owen, 1964) and *Goin' Down the Road* was derailed when, in 1975, the CFDC introduced the Capital Cost Allowance (or the tax shelter programme) which was designed to encourage private investment in Canadian film, but wound up creating a situation not unlike that detailed in Mel Brooks's *The Producers* (1968), with investors actually rooting for films to fail (so that they can write off their entire investments) and producers making awful knock-offs of American movies (particularly disaster movies) featuring faded stars imported from Hollywood. Few of the talented film-makers of the previous decade could get their projects off the ground – and what was made was seldom recognizably Canadian. The decay of urban centres (and urban life) throughout North America also affected the mood of the films. Two

of the best films of the period were Robin Spry's *Drying Up the Streets* (1978) and Daryl Duke's *The Silent Partner* (1978).

Made for the Canadian Broadcasting Corporation by National Film Board veteran Spry, who also made *Flowers on a One Way Street* (1967), and produced by Ralph Thomas (who would later direct *Ticket to Heaven* [1981], an exposé on cults), *Drying Up the Streets* showed a grimy, seedy Toronto where the sex trade flourished and innocents were ruthlessly exploited. The hero is former 1960s radical Pete Brennan (Don Francks) who is recruited (bullied really) by cop Larry (Len Cariou) to help bring down a drug and prostitution ring. Larry hints that Pete's own daughter may be mixed up with the ring. Pete meets Anne (Sarah Togrov), a young girl who reminds him of his daughter and who is under the spell of a spectacularly nasty pimp. Her predicament cuts even closer to the bone as Anne mouths the 1960s platitudes about drugs and self-discovery that Pete helped disseminate.

Blasting away at Toronto's smug self-image as an upright centre for Protestant values, the events of *Drying Up the Streets* take place against the backdrop of rising public anxiety about the tawdry nature of the Yonge Street Strip, an area which stretched from Gerard to around Dundas and was dominated by massage parlours, prostitutes, run-down restaurants, adult bookstores and grindhouses. In August 1977, six months or so after the Toronto Eaton Centre opened, and spurred by the shocking and brutal murder of a young boy named Emanuel Jaques, there was a concerted movement to clean up the Strip. Some politicians used the case to demonize the gay community.

The case also probably influenced the best film noir ever made in English Canada, Daryl Duke's *The Silent Partner*. Sordid, ugly and quite tough-minded, the film was written by American Curtis Hanson, who would go on to make *8 Mile* (2002)

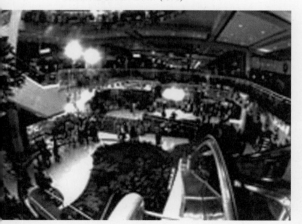

and one of the finest neo-noirs of the late twentieth century, *L.A. Confidential* (1997), and executive produced by Garth Drabinsky, who will found Cineplex and Livent. Perched somewhere between 1970s cynicism and the Hobbesian mindset of the 1980s, *Partner* centres on Miles Cullen (Elliott Gould), a bank clerk/schlemiel who pines for his co-worker Julie Carver (Susannah York), but lacks the gumption to do anything about it. (To further complicate things, she is sleeping with their vile, married boss, Packard [Michael Kirby]).

When a robbery goes horribly wrong, Miles stumbles on a way to scrape off a little something for himself. Unfortunately, the thief, Harry Reikle (Christopher Plummer), is a raging psychopath who takes homicidal umbrage to Miles's entrepreneurial spirit and demands restitution. In one of the film's more memorable scenes, Reikle gets in a gun battle with bank security while wearing a Santa Claus costume and fleeing via a crowded escalator. The cast also includes a pre-*Second City* John Candy and the stunning Celine Lomez as Elaine, a young French woman enlisted/bullied by Reikle into helping set up Miles and who meets her end in one of the period's most Grand Guignol sequences.

Despite, or maybe because of, its scuzzy neo-noir parameters, *Partner* functions as a kind of twisted, refracted history of the period. Forced to dispose of Elaine's remains, Miles tosses them

Blasting away at Toronto's smug self-image as an upright centre for Protestant values, the events of *Drying Up the Streets* take place against the backdrop of rising public anxiety about the tawdry nature of the Yonge Street.

into a construction site which will soon become the vault for the new headquarters for the First Bank of Canada – though it is probably the location of the centre's future parking lot and adjacent to where Drabinsky will open the first Cineplex. *Partner* is very much about the gentrification and corporatization of the city's downtown core, represented by the decidedly grandiose design of the Eaton Centre, a gleaming glass structure clearly influenced by London's fabled Crystal Palace, the architectural emblem for nineteenth-century British colonial and industrial clout. The film's very first shot, a low-angle glimpse of the northernmost part of the building, immediately establishes the mall's importance. Stretching from Dundas Street West to Queen Street West, essentially Toronto's version of Times Square, the Centre was designed to celebrate the grandeur of the Eaton company, one of the oldest retail chains in Canada. Afterwards, similar malls were built across the country.

That same year, following the passage of tougher language laws in Quebec – which placed new restrictions on the use of English by businesses – some of the country's most established companies re-located to Toronto in protest, most notably Sun Life Insurance. These developments eventually helped to make Toronto the country's financial and business centre.

Duke and Hanson provided glimpses of the tawdry underbelly of Toronto through Reikle's world. His favourite hangout is The Silver Dollar Room at Spadina and College, a few blocks north of *The Only Thing You Know*s (Clarke Mackey, 1971) Grossman's. Unlike the real-life club, a venerable blues joint, this version of The Silver Dollar is equipped with backrooms which function as a bawdy house/sauna where friends of the owner can engage in various sordid activities. (Reikle's preferred pastime is beating up young women.)

One of the first films to present Toronto as a liveable city, as a place where difference could be tolerated was *Outrageous!* (Richard Benner, 1977), a low budget drama/comedy about a female impersonator (Craig Russell) and his schizophrenic best friend (Hollis McLaren), directed by the American Benner but produced by the trio who would found the Toronto International Film Festival: Bill Marshall, Henk van der Kolk and Dusty Cohl. The film was a critical and financial hit. Ironically, despite its portrayal of a more cosmopolitan, diverse Toronto, the principals have to escape to New York to realize their dreams. ✣

LOCATIONS MAP
TORONTO

maps are only to be taken as approximates

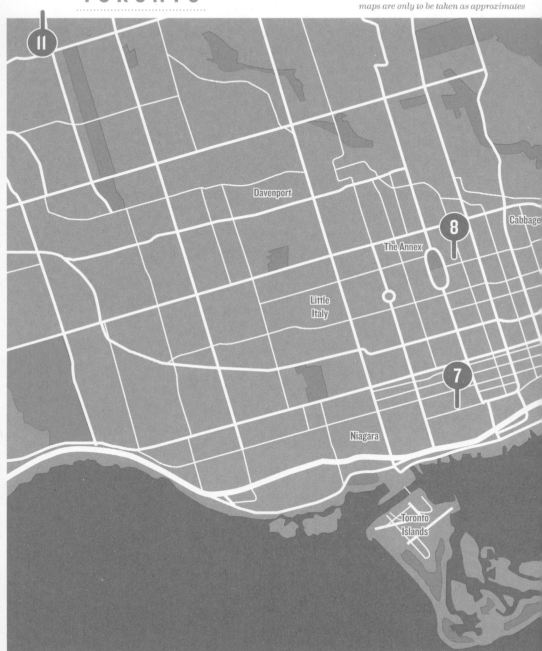

TORONTO LOCATIONS
SCENES 7-12

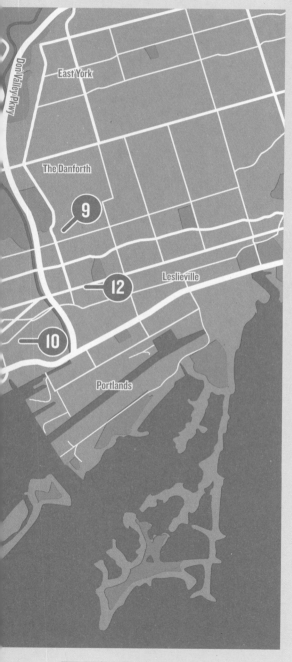

7.
THE KILLING FIELDS (1984)
Fairmont Royal York Hotel,
100 Front Street West
page 28

8.
SHORT CIRCUIT 2 (1988)
Ontario Legislative Building,
111 Wellesley Street West
page 30

9.
COCKTAIL (1988)
Old Don Jail, 14 St Matthews Road
page 32

10.
PERFECTLY NORMAL (1991)
The Canary Restaurant,
409 Front Street East
page 34

11.
BILLY MADISON (1995)
Black Creek Pioneer Village,
1000 Murray Ross Pkwy
page 36

12.
JOHNNY MNEMONIC (1995)
The Opera House, 735 Queen Street East
page 38

THE KILLING FIELDS (1984)

The Fairmont Royal York Hotel, 100 Front Street West

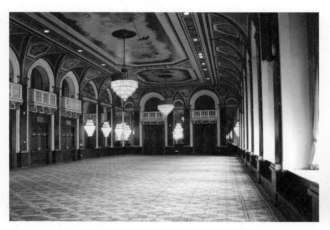
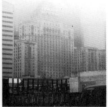

SYDNEY SCHANBERG (Sam Waterson) is accepting the Pulitzer Prize for his journalistic coverage of the fall of Cambodia to the Khmer Rouge. The opulent ballroom, wherein this scene is set, is in fact the Fairmont Royal York Hotel. The marble, heavy fabrics and countless crystal chandeliers provide a decadent setting for Schanberg to speak of Dith Pran (Haing S. Ngor) and the Cambodian victims. The audience, expecting a humble acceptance speech, is instead stunned into a guilty silence in the face of Schanberg's defiant and scathing words. The tall mirrors reflect the shame and futility of those seated in the epitome of safety and affluence. Its magnificence and the contrast between the hotel and the victims are forcibly demonstrated through the juxtaposition of the scene with one of Pran stumbling over a seemingly endless wasteland of skeletons and corpses that he will term the Killing Fields. When the Fairmont Royal York Hotel was built in 1929, it was the tallest building in Canada. It was state of the art, in terms of both luxury and amenities, boasting ten elevators, a 66-foot long switchboard and the country's largest pipe organ. Even though Toronto has a chameleon reputation in film, sometimes it still surprises us. Roland Joffé's powerful and heartrending tale of survival during the Cambodian genocide is about as far from the urban setting as one can imagine. However, it makes the use of the Fairmont Royal York Hotel even more fitting as it provides such a stark contrast to the wretchedness of the Cambodian plight. ↝*Fiona Luck*

Photos © Kevin Harrison

Directed by Roland Joffé

Scene description: Sydney Schanberg's emotional Pulitzer Prize speech credits Dith Pran who is still missing somewhere in the deadly Pol Pot regime

Timecode for scene: 1:42:30 – 1:45:21

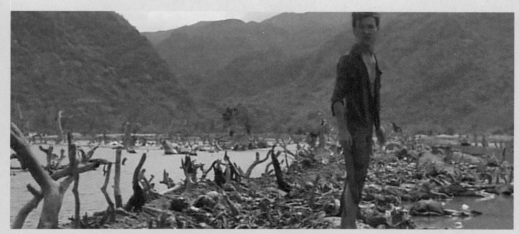

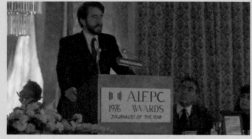

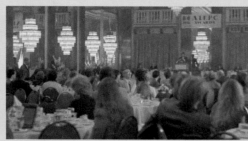

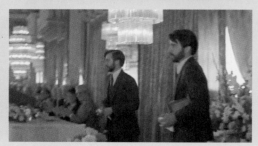

SHORT CIRCUIT 2 (1988)

Ontario Legislative Building, 111 Wellesley Street West

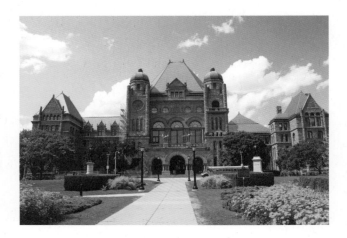

THE LATE-1980S family comedy *Short Circuit 2* is notable for the wholly unconvincing nature of the location filming, which utilizes a variety of well-known areas in downtown Toronto in lieu of its fictional setting, New York City. Over the course of its narrative – which sees sentient robot, Number 'Johnny' Five (Tim Blaney), ultimately succeeding in foiling a bank robbery and gaining nationwide celebrity – numerous prominent Toronto locations are featured, including Dundas Street, Eaton Centre, Bloor Street, Chinatown, and overhead shots of Old City Hall and Berczy Park. The characteristically jingoistic, feel-good climax to the film, in which 'Johnny' Five's sentience is publicly recognized and, alongside numerous other aspiring Americans, he is sworn-in as a US citizen, is filmed in front of the Ontario Legislative Building in Queen's Park (presumably, and improbably, standing in for New York's City Hall). The expansive reverse-shot of the crowd is framed by University Avenue, looking southward towards Front Street West. Little attempt is made to disguise these landmarks for the benefit of the audience, with scarcely more than a tokenistic parade of American flags deployed in an attempt to sustain the illusion. Presumably, the immersive, emotive pull of this sequence, which culminates in 'Johnny' leaping joyously into the air in patriotic celebration of his publicly-enshrined rights and responsibilities, mandated against more thorough (and expensive) attempts at verisimilitude.
⊷Noel Brown

Photo © Kevin Harrison

Directed by Kenneth Johnson
Scene description: Sentient automaton 'Johnny' Five is sworn in as an
American citizen at the film's climax
Timecode for scene: 1:40:50 – 1:42:45

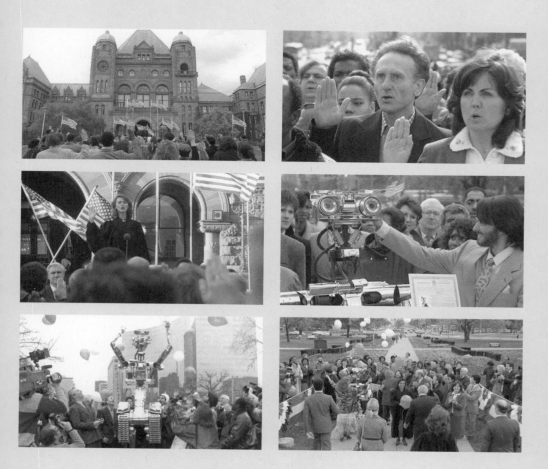

COCKTAIL (1988)

LOCATION

Old Don Jail, 14 St Matthews Road

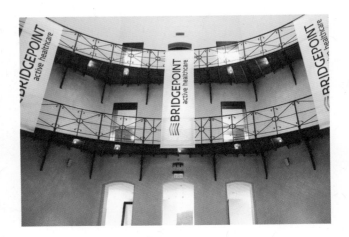

DESPERATION HAS FORCED Brian Flanagan (Tom Cruise) to take a job at a bar but he soon finds that he has a talent for 'flair bartending'. With cynical veteran barkeep friend, Douglas Coughlin (Bryan Brown), Flanagan begins to use their newfound notoriety to raise funds to open their own hotspot. They ply their trade at a nightclub called the Cell Block, which is, in reality, the Rotunda of the Old Don Jail in Toronto's east end. Panopticon in style, the building's round shape with its wrought iron catwalks circling the walls enabled the wardens to see all of the prisoners from the Rotunda. Its vast cavernous size was intended to make inmates feel small and intimidated and this is in keeping with the scene. The muted monochromatic colours and vast domed ceiling loom over Brian. Like inmates in a jail, Brian is caged by social constraints. After countless interviews, he cannot even get a job in a mailroom owing to his lack of work experience and a college degree. The highbrow yuppie clientele line the walls, revelling in their own self-importance, ignoring his attempts to sell drinks, and offering a striking parallel of his failure to break into the corporate world. He panders to this aggressive mob by standing on the bar and spouting a clever yet empty poem, a pattern that he will repeat. *Cocktail* is corny and shallow, yet campy and fun. Despite its poor reviews, it was a box office success and remains a guilty pleasure for many. Today, the Don Jail is the crown jewel of the Bridgepoint Health Center, and it is rumoured to be the most haunted place in Toronto with reports of a distressed spirit floating around the second floor balustrade. Perhaps it saw the film. ⟿*Fiona Luck*

Photo © Kevin Harrison

Directed by Roger Donaldson
Scene description: Brian Flanagan peddles poetry and booze in a trendy nightclub
Timecode for scene: 0:27:14 – 0:31:43

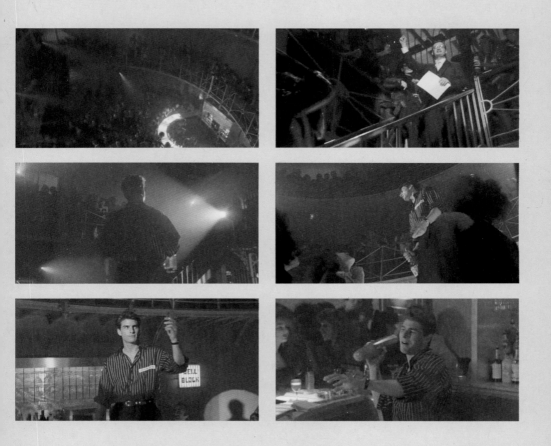

Images © 1988 Touchstone Pictures/Silver Screen Partners III/Interscope Communications

PERFECTLY NORMAL (1991)

LOCATION *The Canary Restaurant, 409 Front Street East*

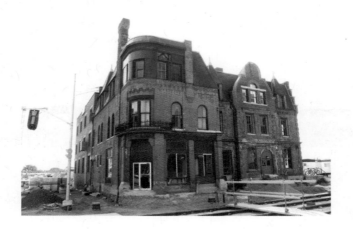

YVES SIMONEAU'S film combines stereotypes of urban Canada to comic effect. The violence of hockey (and a brutal work environment in a beer-bottling plant) is cross-cut by classical music – excerpts from Prokofiev's 'Romeo and Juliet' and the 'Dies Irae' from Verdi's *Requiem* – linking violent sport to melodramatic opera in the shape of an opera-restaurant (now an established phenomenon in many cities but a rarity in 1991), the latest in a series of disastrous culinary ventures on the part of the flamboyant outsider, Alonzo Turner (Robbie Coltrane). We see only the briefest exterior shot of Alonzo's restaurant, setting it in the most decayed part of the inner city. The shot depicts what was originally Palace Street School, erected in 1858 at the intersection of Front and Cherry. Through the twentieth century the building housed a succession of cheap 'flophouse' hotels, with the left-hand end gaining fame as the Canary Restaurant, a 1960s-style diner for industrial and port workers, adorned with Toronto Maple Leafs (hockey) memorabilia. It was threatened with demolition in the late 1980s to make way for a major housing development, hence its down-at-heel appearance when *Perfectly Normal* was made. But, like Alonzo's restaurant, this scheme barely got off the ground. Yet this was not such an unlikely spot for opera. Since 1985, the Canadian Opera Company has had offices, rehearsal facilities and an experimental stage, concentrated in a former gas purifying house and woollen mill, also on Front Street East, a tad nearer downtown. The real Canary Restaurant became a film star in its own right, making cameo appearances in at least nine TV and feature films, variously masquerading as Washington, Boston, Chicago, New York, Detroit and Watertown. Finally closed in 2007, the restaurant building is now scheduled for resurrection as heritage core to a new neighbourhood, to be called ... 'The Canary District'. Where an opera-restaurant failed, a greasy spoon lives on! **➻ Richard Dennis**

Photo © Kevin Harrison

Directed by Yves Simoneau
Scene description: Fresh from injuring his arm in a hockey match, part-time cab driver Renzo
arrives at the building that Alonzo is planning to convert into an opera-restaurant
Timecode for scene: 0:56:04 - 0:56:48

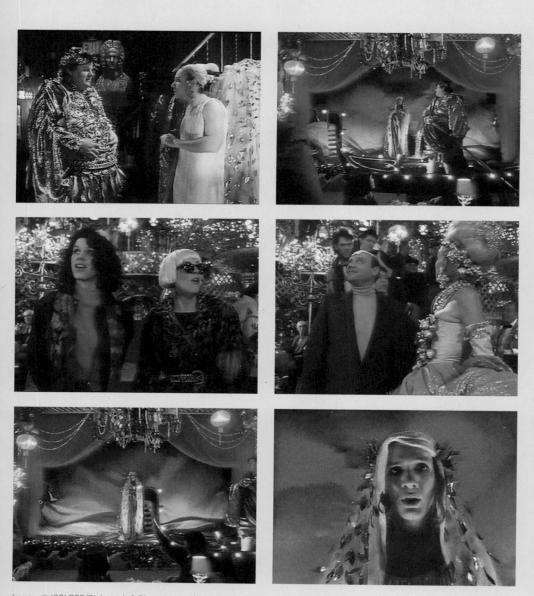

BILLY MADISON (1995)

Black Creek Pioneer Village, 1000 Murray Ross Pkwy

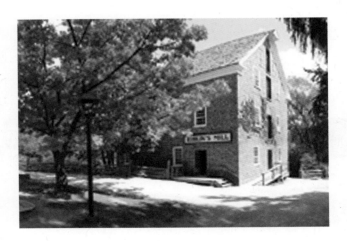

TUCKED AWAY, in the northern edge of Toronto, is the Black Creek Pioneer Village. The venerable Stong family homestead has been augmented over the years with historic buildings from across the province of Ontario – a town hall here, a blacksmith shop there, a mill, a one-room schoolhouse – and employees in costume strolling the grounds, churning butter, weaving and tending to the farm animals. Into this idyll, once strolled Adam Sandler. *Billy Madison* was the comic's leap to the big screen from *Saturday Night Live* (*SNL*, Lorne Michaels, NBC, 1975–). He firmly establishes his man-child persona when he decides to complete grade school in order to impress his father, a retiring business impresario. Sandler's *SNL* partner Chris Farley plays the bus driver who takes Billy, along with his elementary school class, on a trip to the village. Here, he notices that a fellow classmate (age 8, give or take) is crying off in a corner; it turns out that the young man is embarrassed as he has peed his pants. Sandler improvises, tossing water on his own crotch and joking, in front of everyone, about how cool it is to urinate in ones' pants, thus relieving his classmate of his embarrassment. Thus does Sandler win over the hearts of both the school's teacher (Bridgette Wilson-Sampras) and the audience. None of it would have been possible without Toronto's pioneer heritage.
⇢David Fleischer

Directed by Tamra Davis
Scene description: Billy and his class take a trip to the pioneer village
Timecode for scene: 0:42:14 – 0:44:35

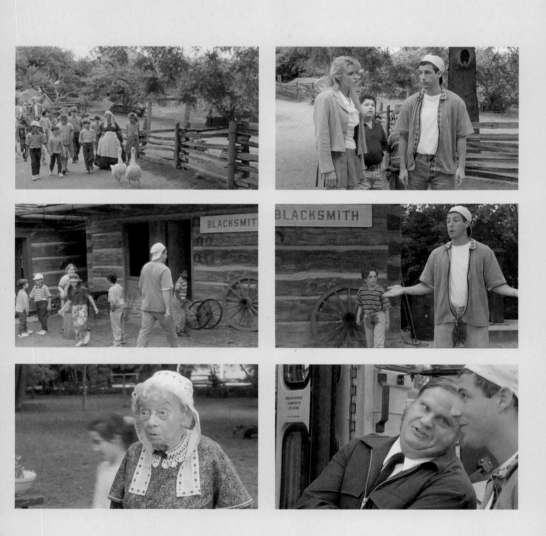

JOHNNY MNEMONIC (1995)

LOCATION *The Opera House, 735 Queen Street East*

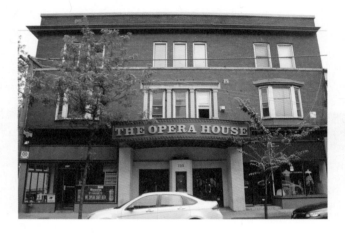

SET IN A DYSTOPIAN NEAR-FUTURE ('New century. Age of Terminal Capitalism') *Johnny Mnemonic* is a loose adaptation of cyberpunk science fiction writer William Gibson's short story of the same title. The film envisions a future in which information politics dominates the world population, and where high-tech virtual reality coexists (for some reason) with VCRs and inexplicably slow fax machines. Johnny, played by Keanu Reeves, is a data courier with a brain implant tasked with the mission of smuggling information encrypted within a fantastical-by-1995 standards 320 gigabytes – data so valuable that pharmaceutical corporations and the yakuza will kill to get their hands on it. In this scene filmed within The Opera House, Johnny suspects that he was set up by Ralfi (Udo Kier) after narrowly escaping an ambush, and he demands answers: 'What did they upload, Ralfi? The goddamned Library of Congress?' Jane (Dina Meyer) then approaches Ralfi for work as a cybernetically-enhanced bodyguard but is refused for being 'damaged goods'. From the table where Ralfi and his fe(male) bodyguards sit, the distinctive balcony area overlooking the stage and floor area of The Opera House is quite recognizable. Fittingly, a techno-gothic blue-haired operatic performance plays in the background. First opened in 1909 as a vaudeville theatre at the corner of Queen Street and Lewis Street, The Opera House also existed for decades as a succession of movie theatres – old film projectors can still be seen in the balcony. Today, it continues to serve as one of Toronto's most historic concert spaces, hosting notable acts such as Rage Against the Machine and Eminem. **•➤ Tyler Shores**

Photo © Kevin Harrison

Directed by Robert Longo

Scene description: Jane approaches Ralfi for bodyguard work at this futuristic techno-punk opera club, and later rescues Johnny from involuntary brain surgery

Timecode for scene: 0:22:24 – 0:24:46

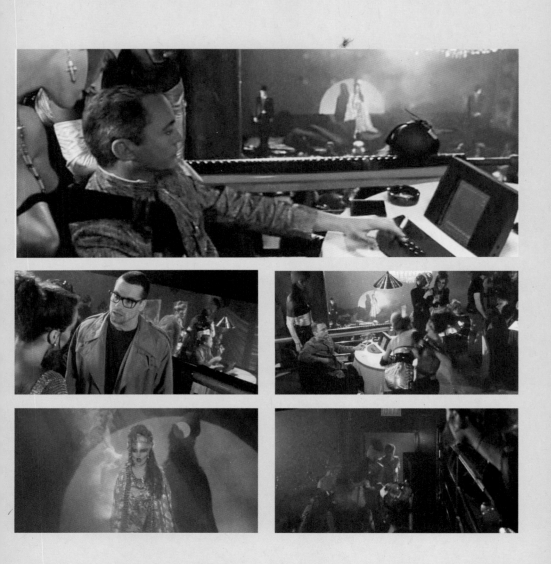

DISTILLING TORONTO HISTORY

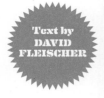

Text by
DAVID
FLEISCHER

How a Victorian Industrial Site Became a Hollywood Backlot

TYPICALLY, IT IS TORONTO'S MIX of urbane but indistinct architecture that has allowed it to successfully play any number of cities in Hollywood productions. So it is somewhat ironic that its distinctive, best-preserved Victorian-era neighbourhood, the Distillery District, has allowed it to do much the same thing. Today, it is a thriving commercial centre, filled with upscale chocolatiers, cafes, galleries and shops. Increasingly, it is flanked by modern, upscale condominiums and populated by well-to-do Torontonians and tourists. It plays host to posh weddings and jazz festivals and you can tour it either on foot or by Segway. But it was not always so. Until quite recently the 14-acre district was effectively terra incognita for local residents, if not for film crews.

The Gooderham and Worts Distillery was founded in 1832, and would become, over the course of that century, the world's single largest producer of spirits ('Distillery District' here and for the remainder of the paragraph). Hard times

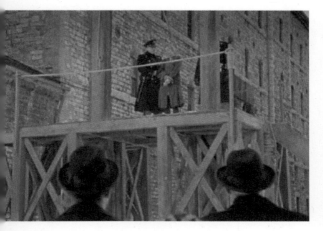

followed in the 1900s, however. World Wars and prohibition took their toll, as did a series of ownership changes. By 1957, whiskey was no longer produced onsite – only rum products. In 1986, the parent company that owned Gooderham and Worts was itself purchased and, in 1990, after 153 years of continued production, the distillery closed its doors. Though it was developed on the shores of Lake Ontario, landfill over the years moved the water to the south and so despite its apparent centrality, the district was geographically isolated. Even if it was not, there was little reason to go there unless one was an architecture buff. Even at its nadir, its distinctive buildings – the red bricks and green doors, the bold limestone hulk of the Stone Distillery – were never fully hidden from view. Toronto's well-driven, elevated Gardiner Expressway passes mere feet away, and a major rail line runs even closer.

In 2003, it reopened as a reclaimed industrial site already familiar from the likes of Chicago's Navy Pier, New York City's South Street Seaport and Baltimore's Inner Harbour. But during that two-decade interregnum, the distillery hosted more than 1,700 film productions, and it became perhaps the single biggest location for film shoots outside of Los Angeles. With distilling operations done, the cobblestone streets and narrow laneways took on many new lives. It became a de facto backlot for dozens of film productions in search of the kind of scenery that is not typically extant in North America.

Look at the opening shots of Bryan Singer's *X-Men* (2000), for example, and you see nothing that remotely suggests Toronto. In the heavy rain, with the addition of some barbed wire and appropriately dressed actors, the distillery easily passes for a Nazi concentration camp. (It

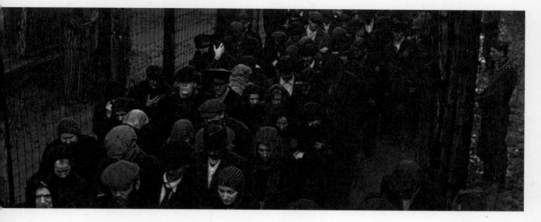

is worth noting that director Matthew Vaughan meticulously re-created this scene for his 'reboot', *X-Men: First Class* (2011) on constructed sets at England's Pinewood Studios. But all Singer needed was set dressing.) At the other end of the tonal scale, the area's gates pass equally well as the Ohio auto parts plant owned by Chris Farley's family in the comedy *Tommy Boy* (Peter Segal, 1995). Combining its ability to play comedy as well as drama and the war elements, the distillery plays an anonymous, war-torn European street during a flashback sequence in the film *Kids in the Hall: Brain Candy* (Kelly Makin, 1996).

Carol Ballard's *The Black Stallion* (1979) is a period piece into which the district fits gracefully. Looking for his runaway horse, the film's young hero, Alec (Kelly Reno), finally gives up in a narrow, foggy alley. From it, almost as in a dream, emerges a man on a cart who happens to have seen the horse. Hovering in the background, visible only in silhouette, is the Stone Distillery, the largest, oldest and most distinctive building in the district. Filmed a generation later, but taking place roughly in the same period, is Academy Award winner for

During that two-decade interregnum, the distillery hosted more than 1,700 film productions, and it became perhaps the single biggest location for film shoots outside of Los Angeles.

Best Picture *Chicago* (Rob Marshall, 2002). It shot not a single frame in its eponymous city, yet here the same distinctive grey building plays the role of a penitentiary exterior. Despite that foreboding cinematic presence, today you can see some of its heritage reclaimed in an on-site

sake distillery, or browse a series of art galleries.

Somewhat more obscurely, the district also played a prison in *Trapped in Paradise* (George Gallo, 1994), starring Nicolas Cage, Jon Lovitz and Dana Carvey. Unsurprisingly, given that it once fronted on the water, it also passes well for a naval yard in the climactic moments of the Al Pacino–Colin Farrell vehicle, *The Recruit* (Roger Donaldson, 2003) and as a New Jersey dockyard in Ron Howard's *Cinderella Man* (2005). More anonymously, its unused interior spaces would host productions like *Three Men and a Baby* (Leonard Nimoy, 1987) and *Frequency* (Gregory Hoblit, 2000).

Outside the district proper are ancillary warehouses and buildings bearing the same architectural imprint. One of the most prominent of these was the Canary Restaurant, a timeless, old-school diner that played itself in dozens of films, including the Jean-Claude Van Damme vehicle *Maximum Risk* (Ringo Lam, 1996) and the rom-com *Three to Tango* (Damon Santostefano, 1999). Today, the restaurant is closed, and the street is a dead-end while the area directly to the east undergoes a massive redevelopment.

This anonymous streetscape can be seen at the end of Edgar Wright's *Scott Pilgrim vs. The World* (2010) as the exterior of the Chaos Theatre, a rare Hollywood film in which Toronto plays itself. The film closes with a final shot from the same location, but with the camera turned 180 degrees. Instead of the dark, closed streetscape to the east, we see the sun setting behind the CN Tower and Toronto's downtown in all its glory. It reminds us that the Distillery District is a world of its own, but still very much a part of the city – especially in its often anonymous role as Hollywood North. ✣

LOCATIONS MAP

TORONTO

maps are only to be taken as approximates

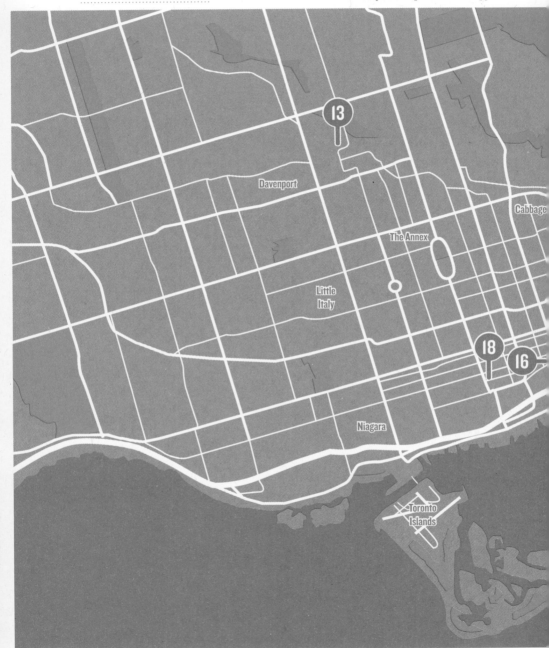

TORONTO LOCATIONS
SCENES 13-18

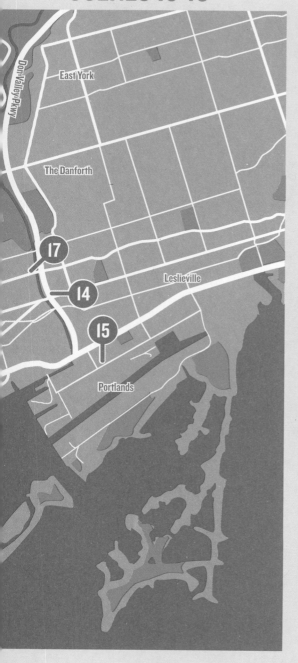

13.
MAXIMUM RISK (1996)
Casa Loma, 1 Austin Terrace
page 44

14.
CRASH (1996)
Don Valley Parkway
page 46

15.
THE SWEET HEREAFTER (1997)
172 Villiers Street (Port Lands);
GO train tracks (present-day Liberty Village);
Lester B. Pearson International Airport
page 48

16.
GOOD WILL HUNTING (1997)
Upfront Bar & Grill, 106 Front Street East
page 50

17.
BLUES BROTHERS 2000 (1998)
Mercedes-Benz Downtown,
761 Dundas Street East
page 52

18.
AMERICAN PSYCHO (2000)
Toronto-Dominion Bank Tower,
66 Wellington Street West
page 54

MAXIMUM RISK (1996)

LOCATION *Casa Loma, 1 Austin Terrace*

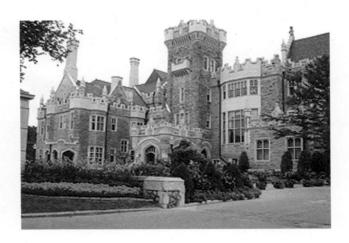

HONG KONG DIRECTOR Ringo Lam joined up with Jean-Claude Van Damme in Lam's North American debut *Maximum Risk*. The genre film sees Van Damme as a French cop who becomes entangled in international espionage, primarily in an ersatz New York City. One of the film's relatively gripping action set-pieces sees Van Damme, clad only in a wrap-around towel, battle baddies in a Russian steam bath. Nothing might seem amiss, but the discerning eye will recognize the distinctive tile-work that belongs to Casa Loma, indisputably the most cinematically endowed domicile in Toronto, if not Canada. In fact, the steam bath is actually the stables of what was once the largest private residence in the country, built on heights just north of downtown. Sir Henry Pellatt made his money at the turn of the twentieth century building hydro-electric facilities and investing in rail lines. World War I slowed construction of his \$3.5-million, 98-room home, complete with a conservatory, secret passages and surrounding gardens. After the war, a depression and other financial difficulties forced Pellatt to sell it to the city after less than a decade as resident. Seventy years later, Casa Loma is a major tourist destination and on-screen it has played everything from the mansion in *X-Men* (Bryan Singer, 2000) to the Ashram run by the titular love guru in Mike Myers's 2008 vehicle (*The Love Guru*, Marco Schnabel).

⇢David Fleischer

Photo © Tom Ue

Directed by Ringo Lam

Scene description: Alain Moreau fights gangsters in a steam bath

Timecode for scene: 0:54:58 – 1:01:36

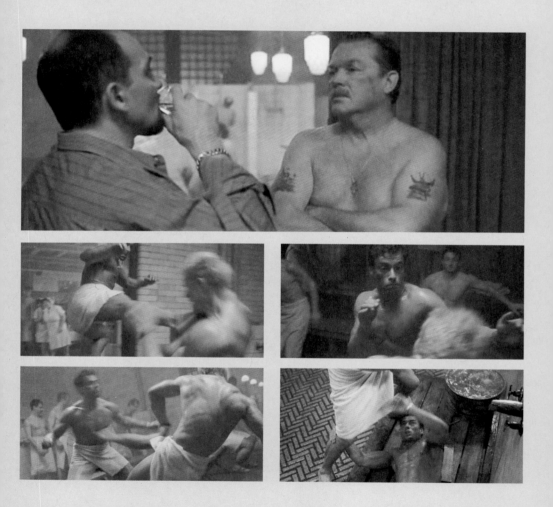

CRASH (1996)

Don Valley Parkway

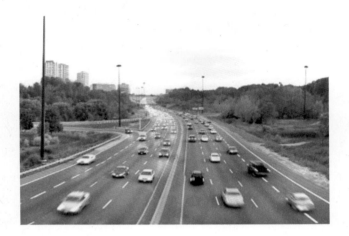

NOT TO BE CONFUSED with Paul Haggis's *Crash* (2004), this complex, disturbing adaptation of J. G. Ballard's 1973 novel delves into the strange netherworld of a group of car crash fetishists obsessed with the erotic possibilities of collision, of the commingling of metal and flesh, 'a liberation of sexual energy that mediates the sexuality of those who have died with an intensity impossible in any other form'. (The conceit is based on the real-life condition of symphorophilia, arousal from the occurrence of disasters.) In this scene, James Ballard (James Spader), his wife Catherine (Deborah Kara Unger) and Vaughan (Elias Koteas) drive the black 1963 Lincoln sedan past a crash scene on the freeway. Vaughan breathlessly takes photos of the wreckage and dazed victims, what he calls 'a work of art ... absolutely a work of art', while the camera fixates upon the distorted forms of twisted metal, smashed glass and broken bodies. The unadorned filming technique, darkly lit atmosphere and hauntingly somber Howard Shore electric guitar score is creepy on a visceral level. Many of the film's scenes were shot along the Don Valley Parkway (DVP), a main traffic corridor serving the downtown Toronto area. On its first day of operation in 1961, the DVP experienced its first traffic jam – an appropriate foreshadowing of its current reputation as one of Toronto's most congested expressways. In fact, characters throughout *Crash* obsessively watch the traffic through binoculars or make prophecies about the gridlock. Helen Remington, for example, observes: 'I had the extraordinary feeling that all these cars were gathering for some special reason I didn't understand. There seemed to be ten times as much traffic.' Interestingly enough, the entirety of the film, according to director David Cronenberg, was shot within a kilometre of his own home. The film notably eschews the type of glamorization found in cinematic car crash scenes: no slow-motion tracking shots, and no explosions, only swift and muted brutality. And yet, the non-descript nature of the freeway scenes is particularly effective – they belong nowhere and anywhere. ➻**Tyler Shores**

Directed by David Cronenberg
**Scene description: A more twisted sort of rubbernecking: James Ballard, Catherine
and Vaughan watch the aftermath of a highway accident
Timecode for scene: 0:57:04 – 1:02:23**

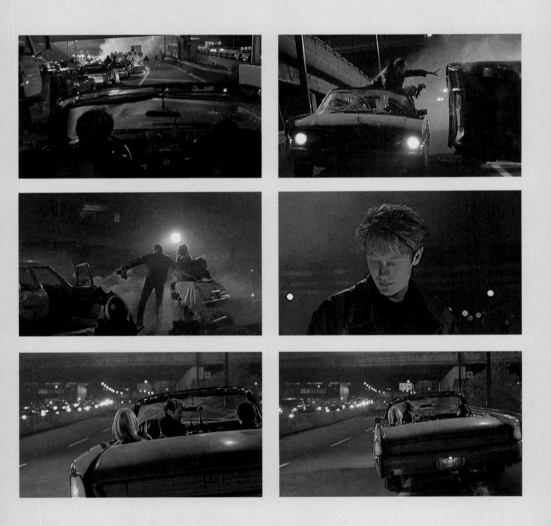

THE SWEET HEREAFTER (1997)

LOCATION *172 Villiers Street (Port Lands)*

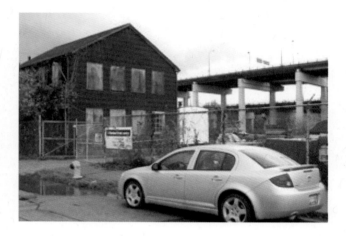

ALTHOUGH ATOM EGOYAN'S *The Sweet Hereafter* takes place mostly in small-town British Columbia (BC), Toronto has an important recurring role. After a school-bus crash near the small town kills almost all the local children, attorney Mitchell Stevens (Ian Holm) arrives hoping to launch a lawsuit on behalf of their grieving parents. But Mitchell has his own lost child, the drug-addicted twenty-something Zoe (Caerthan Banks), who phones her father periodically from Toronto to wheedle money and scream abuse at him. The city is never named, but early on we see Zoe in a car with an iconic GO commuter train passing behind her, and later the Gardiner Expressway appears in the background. Toronto is represented as a place nearly devoid of people, a city of overpasses and desolate parking lots. The vehicles they serve recall the crashed bus in BC and suggest that Zoe has also suffered a kind of death. Near the movie's end, Mitchell arrives at what is identifiably Lester B. Pearson International Airport. There he spots Dolores (Gabrielle Rose), who drove the bus that crashed in BC and was blamed for the accident. Now an exile far from home, she has found work as a hotel shuttle driver. Ferrying guests is presumably a poor substitute for the work with children that she loved, and we realize that Toronto has become a bittersweet hereafter for her. Dolores has crossed Canada to gain anonymity in a city that, as the movie depicts it, is also both anonymous and recognizable, an open secret.

⇢ Robert McGill

Photo © Robert McGill

Scene description: : Zoe calls her father from the Port Lands with the Gardiner Expressway behind her
Timecode for scene: 1:20:10 - 1:22:14

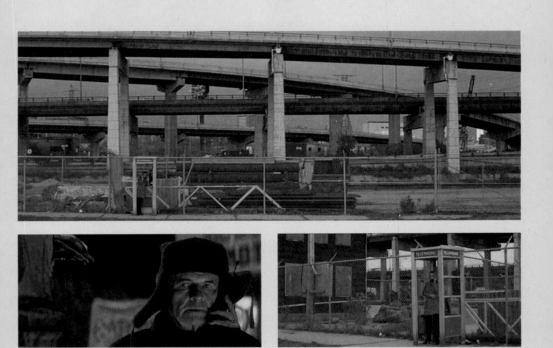

GOOD WILL HUNTING (1997)

LOCATION *Upfront Bar & Grill, 106 Front Street East*

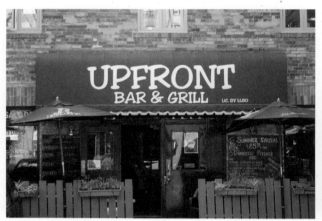

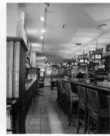

TORONTO GIVES A CONVINCING impression of Boston in *Good Will Hunting*. When Massachusetts Institute of Technology janitor and math savant Will Hunting (Matt Damon) travels with friends to Cambridge, Massachusetts, the exterior shot provides a brief glimpse of the Bow and Arrow Pub, at the time a popular student hangout located in Harvard Square. Interior shots were filmed entirely in Toronto's Upfront Bar & Grill, including the memorable bar scene where Will first meets Skyler (Minnie Driver) while putting down a 'Michael Bolton clone' graduate student for regurgitating Gordon Wood and Vickers: 'Do you have any thoughts of your own on this matter? Or ... is that your thing, you come into a bar, read some obscure passage and then pretend, you pawn it off as your own idea just to impress some girls, embarrass my friend?' The scene is parodied, with Damon and Affleck reprising the leads in a make-believe 'Good Will Hunting 2' in Kevin Smith's *Jay and Silent Bob Strike Back* (2001). Trivia fans might also note that the famous 'How do you like them apples?' scene was shot a few doors down at a Dunkin' Donuts on Massachusetts Avenue. For a suitably New England vibe, the Upfront was decorated with a prominent American flag, Boston Red Sox, Celtics and Bruins sports memorabilia adorning the walls. Located just east of St Lawrence Market in the heart of Toronto's Old Town neighbourhood, the brown-brick Upfront Bar & Grill is a Toronto sports and watering hole mainstay. In addition to its local reputation for chicken wings, the restaurant proudly keeps Boston mementos from its movie appearances in *Good Will Hunting* and the romantic comedy *Fever Pitch* (Bobby Farrelly, 2005). ➦ *Tyler Shores*

Photos © Kevin Harrison

Directed by Gus van Sant

**Scene description: Will Hunting first meets Skyler at a 'Harvard Bar' while lecturing
a graduate student on the follies of quoting Vickers and Wood
Timecode for scene: 0:15:47 – 0:21:25**

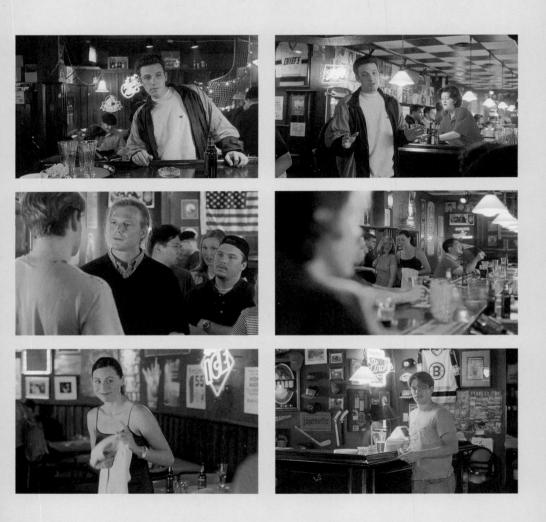

BLUES BROTHERS 2000 (1998)

LOCATION *Mercedes-Benz Downtown, 761 Dundas Street East*

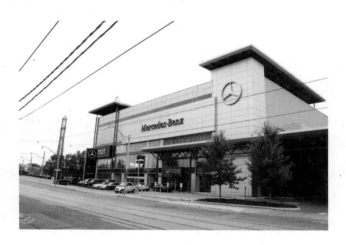

DAN AYKROYD'S INSPIRATION for the band The Blues Brothers stemmed largely from his formative years spent in the Canadian capital city of Ottawa. Nevertheless, whilst *The Blues Brothers* (John Landis, 1980) was shot in Chicago and felt authentic, *The Blues Brothers 2000* uses sparsely decorated studio stages and disguised Toronto landmarks, as stand-ins for the Windy City. *2000* comes alive in the glimpses when Toronto is surreptitiously involved. Cherry Street, Lakeshore Boulevard and the Markham Fairgrounds are backdrops to some of the film's most memorable moments, but the most conspicuous use of the city occurs at the Mercedes-Benz Downtown dealership. The showroom is entirely authentic and functional, built in 1992 with a contemporary glass-and-steel design and set beside the Don River with a view of the bustling Don Valley Parkway and beyond. With a breathtaking level of product-placement, in *2000*, the modern design of the dealership becomes a musical stage where Mrs Murphy (Aretha Franklin) and her coterie of brightly coloured shopping companions reprise a familiar scene from the original *Blues Brothers*, lecturing Matt Murphy with their demand for 'Respect'. Despite the stilted dialogue, the actors/singers are clearly enjoying themselves as Murphy not only grins throughout his performance, but his head bobs in time to the music, whilst Franklin goes 'full Diva' at him with a barely concealed sparkle in her eyes. Furthermore, the genuine Downtown location offers one of the few bright and light-hearted scenes in *2000*, the rest of which comprises seedy strip-clubs, prisons, apocalyptic music festivals and Voodoo palaces. **↝ Carl Wilson**

Photo © Kevin Harrison

Directed by John Landis
Scene description: Elwood Blues takes his band to a car dealership
in (a familiar) attempt to re-enlist one of their past members
Timecode for scene: 0:32:01 – 0:38:01

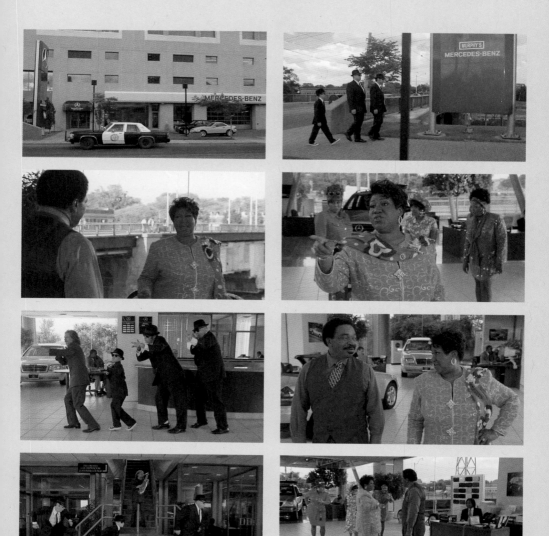

AMERICAN PSYCHO (2000)

LOCATION

Toronto-Dominion Bank Tower, 66 Wellington Street West

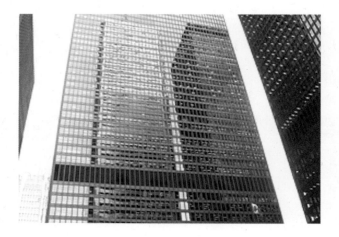

THE CAMERA LOOKS in on a spacious high-rise office, where five men in clean suits crowd around an oak table. Patrick Bateman (Christian Bale), an investment banker at New York's Pierce & Pierce, removes a silver holder from his coat and flips the top to reveal a cream-coloured business card. The location is actually the Toronto-Dominion Bank Tower, one of six buildings that comprise the Toronto-Dominion Centre. The Centre headquarters Toronto-Dominion Bank, a multinational financial corporation and the second largest bank in Canada. With its black steel beams and mirror-like windows, the complex resembles a pre-9/11 World Trade Center, rendering it a perfect stand-in for a film critiquing New York's finance industry: *American Psycho* probes the vanity of 1980s investment banking, offering a stringent censure of the careerism and egomania that led to that recession – and, coincidentally, the current one. Bateman places the card on the table, slides it confidently toward his colleagues, and says, suavely, 'New card.' His so-called friends, all of whom possess slightly nicer cards, quickly outdo Bateman, who goes green with envy. Ironically, the cards are almost identical, revealing the petty scrutiny under which these men live, and where Bateman, a murdering thrill-seeker and certifiable sociopath, thrives. **◆John James**

Photo © Kevin Harrison

Directed by Mary Harron
Scene description: Bateman flaunts business cards with colleagues
Timecode for scene: 0:12:26 – 0:15:27

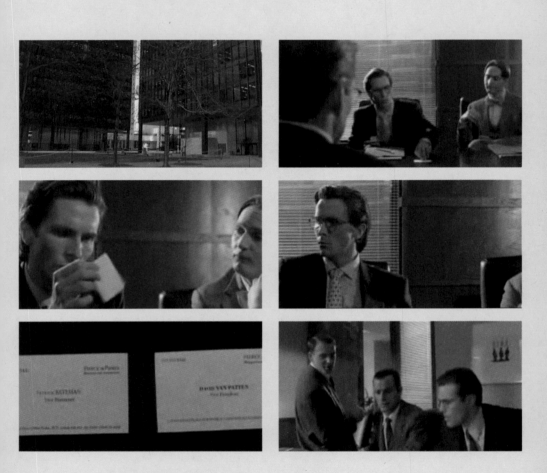

THE TORONTO NEW WAVE

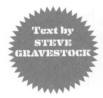

Text by
STEVE
GRAVESTOCK

THE TORONTO NEW WAVE was a loosely affiliated group of film-makers who emerged in the mid-1980s. Patricia Rozema's charming debut feature *I've Heard the Mermaids Singing* (1987) was not the first film from the New Wave – that honour would go to Atom Egoyan's *Next of Kin* (1984) – but it established the movement, in part, because of its international and domestic success. Emerging after the myriad failures of the tax shelter years with their woefully inadequate imitations of American genre work and funded primarily through arts councils as opposed to Telefilm, these film-makers had little interest in the documentary/ realist tradition advocated by the National Film Board and those it trained, and they had direct ties to the local Toronto theatre scene and the burgeoning avant-garde scene of the 1980s.

For instance, Peter Lynch, a key film-maker in the New Wave who was responsible for the much celebrated *Project Grizzly* (1996), and who directed Don McKellar in one of his most memorable turns in the short 'Arrowhead' (1992), was co-founder of Video Culture International, a festival which hosted artists including Nam June Paik and Bill

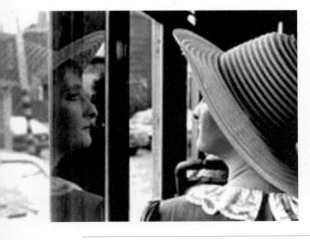

Viola. McKellar, along with Tracey Wright and Daniel Brooks, founded the avant-garde theatre troupe, the Augusta Company.

The links to the artist community are both acknowledged and satirized in Rozema's film. Polly Vandersma (Sheila McCarthy), a naïve young woman who earns her living as a temp girl or rather 'person Friday', gets a job at the Church Gallery, owned and curated by Gabrielle (veteran Quebecois film-maker and actress Paule Baillargeon). A committed amateur photographer, Polly takes an immediate shine to 'the Curator' because, in Polly's words, 'She was one of those people you see in restaurants talking and inter … facing' – activities for which the always awkward Polly has little facility. Gabrielle represents a world Polly knows little about, but as the film proceeds it becomes clear that she is all image and no show, more conversant with artspeak jargon than painting. (The movie argues that Polly is a more genuine artist.) Polly realizes this herself when she accidentally overhears Gabrielle and her lover Mary (played by playwright and author Ann-Marie MacDonald) confess to fraud. It turns out that Mary did the paintings which Gabrielle, albeit unintentionally, has been exhibiting as her own. The film rather perfectly captures the ethos of the period when Toronto saw itself as hip and wised-up (conversant with cutting-edge developments in a variety of artistic fields) but also naïve, awkward and inexperienced.

Here Toronto is cold, uptight and judgmental (see the Curator) but also a place that can nurture people like Polly, whose imagination flies even amidst the glassy corporate office towers of Bay Street. The Toronto Eaton Centre figures prominently here as well, again from the first shot, but it is used somewhat contrapuntally. When Polly goes to interview for the temp job, she enters through the Yonge Street doors but exits on the other side to find a quaint and centuries-

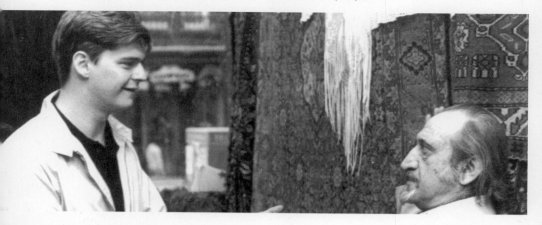

old church nestled behind the mall – the location of Gabrielle's gallery. The corporatization of the cityscape predicted in *The Silent Partner* (Daryl Duke, 1978) is, by this point, a done deal, but somehow eccentric pockets still exist like the Church Gallery and Polly's strange little apartment building, which is situated between more conventional houses and a factory spewing toxins.

I've Heard the Mermaids Singing premiered at Cannes as part of the Director's Fortnight, causing a huge stir and eventually selling to a then small American company which specialized in independent films: Miramax. It did phenomenally on its home turf as well, running for months at Toronto's Carlton Cinemas, at the time, the city's major art house theatre. The title, incidentally, comes from T. S. Eliot.

One of the traits that distinguished the Toronto New Wave was their emphasis on geographic specificity and their interest in ethnic (and decidedly non-corporate) enclaves. The upper-classed hero of Egoyan's *Next of Kin* flees his real family to masquerade as the long lost son of an Armenian Canadian family. The patriarch runs a clothing store in Kensington Market, an ethnically-diverse neighbourhood which has long been a lightning rod and rite of passage for the city's bohemians as well as a sort of protest to the 'white bread' official image of Toronto – and probably Victoria, where Egoyan grew up.

> **One of the traits that distinguished the Toronto New Wave was their emphasis on geographic specificity and their interest in ethnic (and decidedly non-corporate) enclaves.**

Twitch City (1998–2000), the CBC-produced sitcom written by Don McKellar and directed and produced by Bruce McDonald, is also set in Kensington. McKellar plays a TV-obsessed shut-in who spends his days watching bombastic American style talk shows à la Jerry Springer and Geraldo Rivera.

Bruce McDonald's 1989 debut feature, *Roadkill*, opens with its heroine (Valerie Buhagiar) experiencing the annual Easter Parade in Toronto's Little Italy – possibly a sign of her imminent awakening and maturation.(Ironically, despite the fact that he is possibly the director most identified with the city, McDonald did not shoot another recognizable Toronto exterior until *This Movie is Broken* [2010].) The unilingual and privileged hero (Sean Astin) of Jerry Ciccoritti's underrated romantic comedy *Boy Meets Girl* (1998) is rescued by a chance encounter with a mysterious girl (the luminous Emily Hampshire) who does not speak a word of English – and possibly by the vitality of Little Italy itself. By contrast, in the aforementioned 'Arrowhead', Don McKellar's chatty Ray escapes the lifeless concrete monstrosity of the Don Mills apartment building that he lives in by exploring the nearby Don Valley. In some films, abandoned industrial spaces house and nurture rebels (see Peter Mettler's 1989 *Top of His Head*, where the anti-corporate artist activists hang out and plot in an abandoned warehouse) and the disenfranchised (for instance, the neglected kids in Jeremy Podeswa's *The Five Senses* (1999) take refuge in an empty factory).✤

NOTE: See also the model home in Egoyan's *The Adjuster* (1992) and the ramshackle house, situated between two highway ramps, that is occupied by the two social misfits in Vincenzo Natali's absurdist comedy *Nothing* (2003).

LOCATIONS MAP
TORONTO

maps are only to be taken as approximates

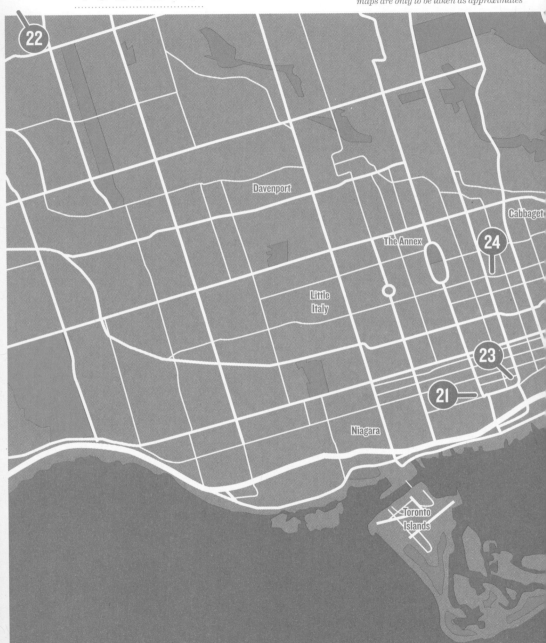

22

Davenport

Cabbaget

The Annex

24

Little
Italy

23

21

Niagara

Toronto
Islands

TORONTO LOCATIONS
SCENES 19-24

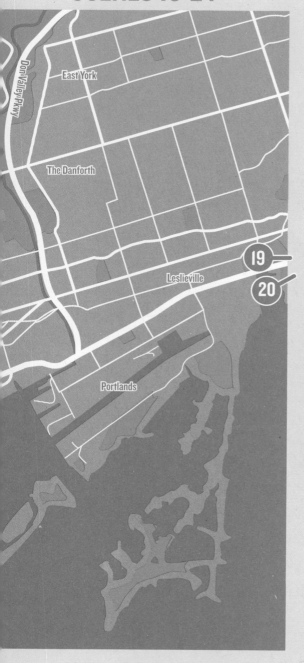

19.
THE SKULLS (2000)
Greek Theatre at Guild Inn and Gardens,
201 Guildwood Parkway
page 60

20.
FREQUENCY (2000)
Garden Gate Restaurant (The Goof),
2379 Queen Street East
page 62

21.
X-MEN (2000)
Roy Thomson Hall, 60 Simcoe Street
page 64

22.
GINGER SNAPS (2000)
Scarlett Heights Entrepreneurial Academy,
15 Trehorne Drive
page 66

23.
WES CRAVEN PRESENTS:
DRACULA 2000 (2000)
Merchants' Bank building
(also known as the Heritage building),
Allen Lambert Galleria, Brookfield Place
(formerly BCE Place), 181 Bay Street
page 68

24.
DEATH TO SMOOCHY (2002)
Maple Leaf Gardens, 60 Carlton Street
page 70

THE SKULLS (2000)

Greek Theatre at Guild Inn and Gardens, 201 Guildwood Parkway

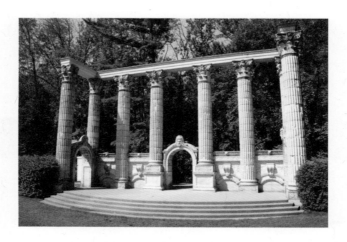

THE SKULLS IS A CAUTIONARY THRILLER that explores a fictionalized version of the famous Skull and Bones society, the secret organization at Yale to which three US presidents belonged. Unlike Caleb Mandrake (Paul Walker), who, as the son of the opportunistic and conniving Judge Litten Mandrake (Craig T. Nelson) was 'born a Skull', Luke McNamara (Joshua Jackson) is drafted into the society on his own merits. Thus begins the rather convoluted exploration of the film's themes of wealth, status and integrity. Romanesque portions of the University of Toronto's architecture, which stands in for Yale, provide an underused but elegant backdrop to the frequently vapid action of the plot, as locations like the stately Knox Chapel and neo-gothic University College serve little purpose beyond background to the characters' alternating smoldering and smugness. On the other hand, Scarborough's Guild Inn, a former artists' colony that is now the site of a sculpture garden, provides a literal stage for the film's climactic scene, when, after falling victim to the elder Mandrake's machinations, Luke challenges Caleb to a pistol duel. The Inn's Greek Theatre features white Corinthian columns – rescued from the Bank of Toronto's 1966 demolition – surrounding a raised stone stage, and it is an ideal location for settling a score within a secret society whose roots date back to the early 1800s. Its classically inspired Zeus-like bas-relief, a silent observer presiding over the scene, exudes an enduring power and moral permanence that transcends the pettiness of human drama, even among the elite. •*Georgia Rushing Macey*

Photo © Kevin Harrison

Directed by Rob Cohen
Scene description: *Luke and Caleb meet in a duel with the other Skulls as witnesses*
Timecode for scene: *1:33:52 – 1:36:15*

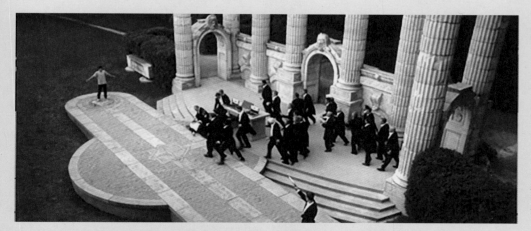

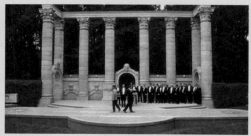

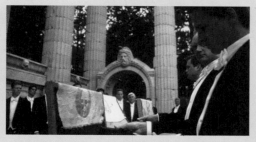

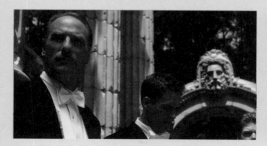

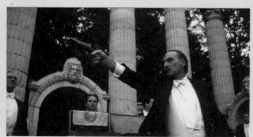

FREQUENCY (2000)

LOCATION *Garden Gate Restaurant (The Goof), 2379 Queen Street East*

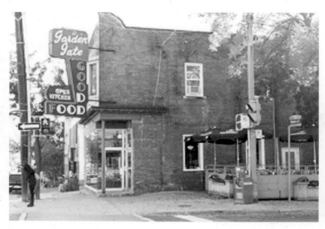
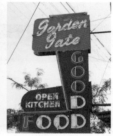

ON ITS SURFACE, *Frequency* is a complexly plotted science fiction mystery, but at heart, it is the story of a family shaped by tragedy and how the powers of love and hope can change fate. The only scene in which characters other than father and son Frank (Dennis Quaid) and John Sullivan (Jim Caviezel) encounter the transformative magic of history being rewritten is when family friend and NYPD detective Satch (Andre Braugher) takes Julia Sullivan (Elizabeth Mitchell) to a diner to explain over coffee why Frank has been detained for questioning. The diner is Toronto's Garden Gate Restaurant, fondly known as The Goof, which stands in for a late-1960s period diner in Queens where locals gather to eat. As Satch breaks the news to Julia, he is distracted by the World Series game playing behind the counter, as he sees it unfolding exactly the way Frank told him it would. Julia cannot understand why Satch keeps cutting off – and eventually abandoning – his explanation, but as Satch's normally severe expression is replaced by one of astonishment, it becomes clear that he must suspend his scepticism and embrace the fact that Frank's outlandish tale of his grown son reaching back through time to save lives may actually be the truth. The diner provides a setting for the film's theme, played out by both the historic events of the Amazin' Mets' World Series win as well as the human drama of the Sullivan family, that miracles can happen any time, anywhere. ⇢*Georgia Rushing Macey*

Photos © Fiona Luck

Directed by Gregory Hoblit

Scene description: Satch tries to explain to Jules why he has arrested Frank,
but gets distracted by the ball game on television
Timecode for scene: 1:32:47 – 1:38:53

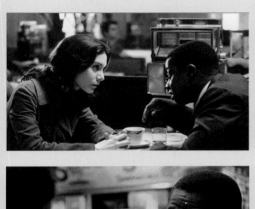 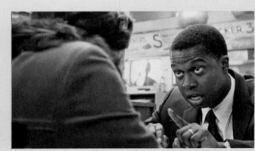

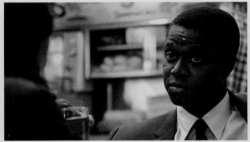 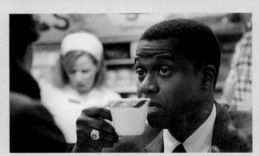

X-MEN (2000)

Roy Thomson Hall, 60 Simcoe Street

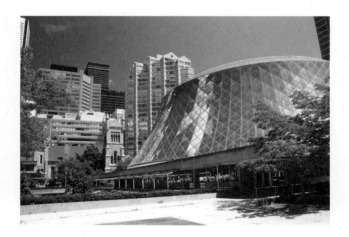

THE INFLUX OF COMIC BOOK MOVIES in recent years owes much to Bryan Singer's *X-Men*. Despite its superheroic trappings, the film is grounded in a very real humanistic philosophy about mutants who grapple with the societal prejudices leveled against those who are different. Immediately following an anti-mutant US Senate hearing, we see this early important exchange between Professor Charles Xavier (Patrick Stewart) and Magneto (Ian McKellen), which was filmed in the lobby of Toronto's Roy Thomson Hall. The conversation introduces the conflicting ideologies – between peaceful coexistence, and war between mutants (homo sapiens superior) and mankind – that set the tone for the rest of the *X-Men* films. With its distinctive honeycombed glass canopy of steel and glass, the design of Roy Thomson Hall well-characterizes the scene: Xavier in the sunlight, Magneto in the shadows (note also the intersecting Xs visible in the background). Hinting at the lengths to which he is willing to go, Magneto leaves Xavier: 'We are the future, Charles, not them. They no longer matter.' Formerly known as New Massey Hall, the current Roy Thomson Hall and its curved glass design is one of downtown Toronto's most recognizable structures. Since its opening in 1982 and through its massive 2002 renovation, it has become renowned as one of Canada's premier concert venues. During its eventful history, the Hall has hosted some of the music world's greatest performers and is home to the Toronto Symphony Orchestra. As a major venue for arts and entertainment events, the Roy Thomson Hall is a symbol of the city's prominence in the world's cultural stage. •◦ ***Tyler Shores***

Photo © Kevin Harrison

Directed by Bryan Singer
Scene description: Ideologies of war and peace clash as Professor Charles Xavier and Magneto
debate the future of human and mutant kind in this early and important scene
Timecode for scene: 0:08:10 – 0:09:22

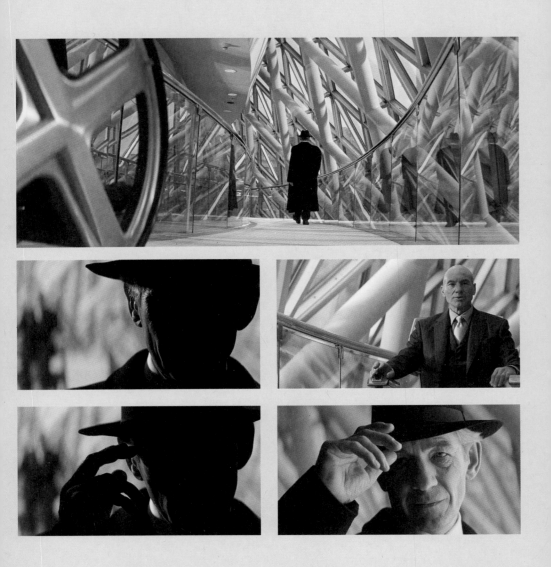

GINGER SNAPS (2000)

Scarlett Heights Entrepreneurial Academy, 15 Trehorne Drive

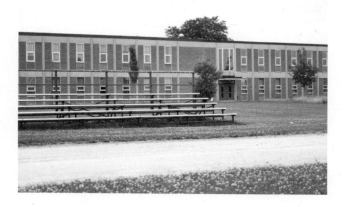

WAITING FOR THEIR GYM CLASS field hockey shift, *Ginger Snaps*'s death-obsessed protagonists, the Fitzgerald sisters (Emily Perkins and Katharine Isabelle), express displeasure with their surroundings: Brigitte (Perkins) calls high school a 'hormonal toilet... I'd rather wait it all out in our room'. The contrast between the high school and the Fitzgerald sisters' bedroom is important. The former is a real school, Etobicoke's Scarlett Heights Entrepreneurial Academy; the latter is a film set designed to reflect their personalities. Director John Fawcett says that the suburbs represent 'the horror of banality'. He chose the school partly due to its lack of aesthetic value. Yet while the real Scarlett Heights requires uniforms, a symbol of banality/conformity, it is actually ethnically diverse with unique programs emphasizing experiential learning. The pale exterior of Scarlett Heights suggests a bland world the Fitzgeralds seek to avoid, but it may hide a vibrant world encouraging difference. Teenage pessimism can be misplaced, which Brigitte learns when Ginger's angst is manifested in violence. The supposed banality of the world outside the Fitzgeralds' room is mirrored by suburban sprawl. *Ginger Snaps* was released two years after the amalgamation that merged Toronto and surrounding cities into one 'mega-city'. It captures a then-new suburban aspect of Toronto. The film's residential scenes were shot in Brampton, a segment of the now-Greater Toronto Area that was, like Etobicoke, previously independent. The houses share the school's pale beige, dark red and orange colour scheme, implicitly linking both cities in a long suburban sprawl of conformity, from which the Fitzgerald sisters retreat into artifice. **⇢Michael Da Silva**

Photo © Kevin Harrison

Directed by John Fawcett
Scene description: Ginger is oggled during field hockey while she and Brigitte moan about high school
Timecode for scene: 0:07:53 – 0:09:18

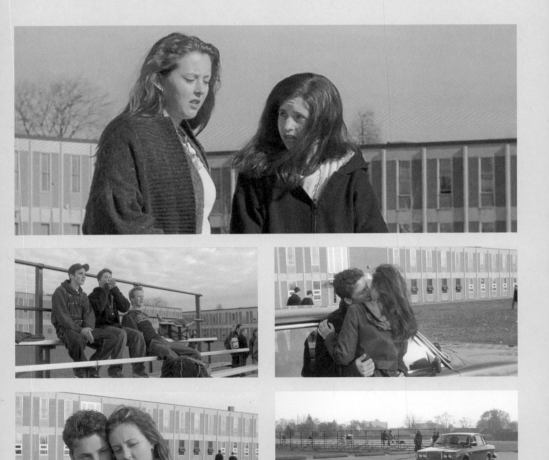

WES CRAVEN PRESENTS: DRACULA 2000 (2000)

Merchants' Bank building (also known as the Heritage building), Allen Lambert Galleria, Brookfield Place (formerly BCE Place), 181 Bay Street

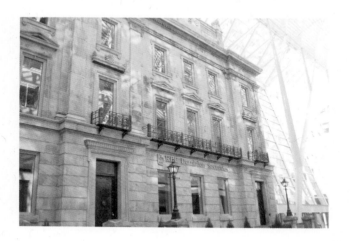

CARFAX, DRACULA'S LONDON ABODE, has always been essential to his story. In Bram Stoker's 1897 novel, it is the estate that Dracula purchases, an old house surrounded by trees with a chapel nearby. In Tod Browning's 1931 film, the estate and chapel merge into Carfax Abbey, a name upheld by Francis Ford Coppola in his 1992 reimagining. For *Dracula 2000*, director Patrick Lussier opts to modernize and urbanize Carfax. Now Carfax Antiques, it is recast as Van Helsing's (Christopher Plummer) London office, and Dracula (Gerard Butler) is locked in a steel coffin deep within its high-security crypt. Lussier selects as this new Carfax the nineteenth-century facade of the Merchants' Bank building, which, having survived Toronto's 1904 fire, has been moved from its original location on 13–15 Wellington Street West, restored, and reassembled beside the escalator to the subway station in the Allen Lambert Galleria. The antique business and its antiquated facade sharply contrast the Galleria's ultra-modern glass-and-steel six-storey-high parabolic frame, which was built to suggest a forest canopy – although its height and design equally evoke a medieval gothic cathedral. Lussier's Carfax thus incorporates Stoker's trees, church and aged safe-haven for Dracula's coffin, but alters the resulting image. Van Helsing is the antique here, not Dracula. Simon's (Jonny Lee Miller) leaving the office and descending into the subway contrasts Marcus's (Omar Epps) breaking in and anticipates the thieves' descent into Van Helsing's vaults. They greedily abscond with the coffin without knowing its contents, unleashing Dracula, who is uniquely no longer tied to Carfax for survival. **◆Sheri Chriqui**

Photo © Sheri Chriqui

Directed by Patrick Lussier
Scene description: Thieves enter Carfax
Timecode for scene: 0:05:34 – 0:07:36

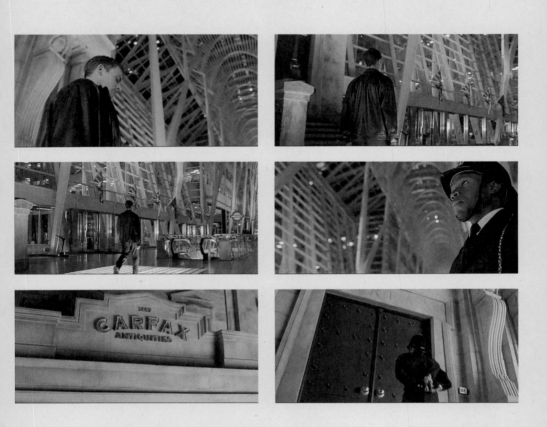

DEATH TO SMOOCHY (2002)

LOCATION *Maple Leaf Gardens, 60 Carlton Street*

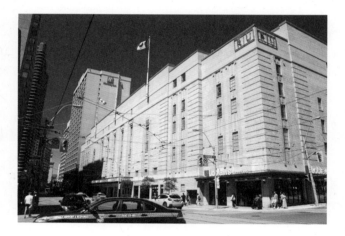

REVENGE, MURDER AND INTRIGUE converge at Maple Leaf Gardens in the climactic ice show scenes of *Death to Smoochy*. Sheldon Mopes (Edward Norton) gains fame as Smoochy the Rhino, a wholesomely goofy children's television host who replaces the manic and disgraced 'Rainbow Randolph' Smiley (Robin Williams). The over-the-top ice opera of 'Smoochy on Ice' – complete with Nazis, Fellini-esque little people in masks and Madame Butterfly melody – can lay claim to being one of the weirder moments in the Maple Leaf Gardens's history. Built in 1931 over an astonishingly rapid six months, the stately domed structure was fondly known by fans as 'the Cathedral of Ice Hockey' and it was home to the Toronto Maple Leafs for almost seven decades. The Gardens were arguably the city's most important entertainment venue with its rich legacy: home to a dozen Canadian sports teams; site of the first ever National Basketball Association game; and location for a multitude of social and cultural events including the likes of Muhammad Ali, Elvis Presley, Frank Sinatra, The Beatles, Winston Churchill and many, many others. Despite being named a Historic Site of Canada in 2007, the Gardens would lay unused until 2011. Today, the location serves as a multiple-purpose building, with Ryerson University's Mattamy Athletic Centre occupying the upper level, and Loblaw's massive 85,000-square foot flagship grocery store, the ground level. The building is replete with artful reminders and plaques commemorating its cultural history (including a spot marking the centre of the ice from the old arena) and fittingly enough, the upper floor contains a 2,600-seat hockey rink for the Ryerson University Rams hockey team. **➻ Tyler Shores**

Photo © Kevin Harrison

Directed by Danny DeVito
Scene description: Sheldon Mopes is rescued from a mob hit by Randolph during the film's climactically weird 'Smoochy on Ice' scene
Timecode for scene: 1:30:23 – 1:37:48

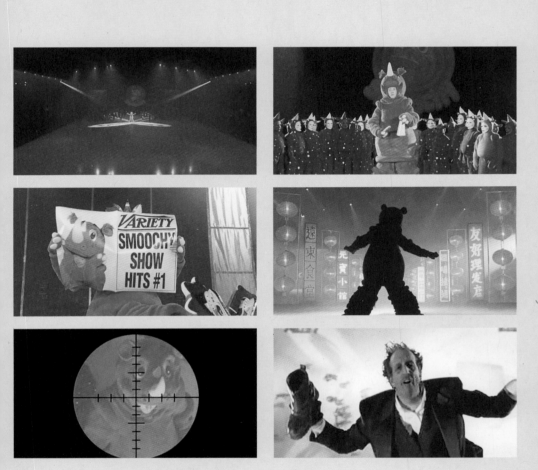

AT HOME IN TORONTO

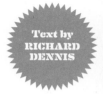

Text by RICHARD DENNIS

Houses and Apartments that Signify the City

IN MOST FILMS made in Toronto, in which the city is pretending to be somewhere else, usually Washington or New York or Chicago or Boston, but sometimes less flattering aliases like Detroit, or any town that looks generically North American rather than specifically Canadian, the last place that a director will want to show is a location so 'typical' of Toronto that it could hardly be anywhere else: late-Victorian 'bay and gable' or Cabbagetown cottage rows with mansard roofs or steep-pitched, front-facing gables over the doors. For films that make a virtue of being set in Toronto, these features are a must. In *Take this Waltz* (Sarah Polley, 2011), Margot (Michelle Williams) lives in 'McLaughlin Crescent, near Queen and Dufferin', in real life, 62 Mackenzie Crescent, 'Beaconsfield Village', just north-east of Queen and Dufferin. In the teen fantasy comedy,

Scott Pilgrim vs. the World (Edgar Wright, 2010), Scott (Michael Cera) lives on 'Albert Avenue', in reality Alberta Avenue, Wychwood, a tree-lined street of early twentieth-century houses with substantial porches and dormer windows and, in a few cases, garages underneath houses set back and above the level of the sidewalk; but Ramona's (Mary Elizabeth Winstead) home is a classic Victorian 'bay-and-gable' on Carlton Street, Cabbagetown. Carlton – this time more modest row housing but still with Toronto gables – also looks the likely home of the criminal Harry Reikle (Christopher Plummer), who lives at '11 Winston Street', in Cabbagetown', in *The Silent Partner* (Daryl Duke, 1978). But *Partner* also offers us another distinctive residential environment, a three-storey-plus-basement walk-up apartment house, fronted with wooden verandas, occupied in the film by Miles Cullen (Elliott Gould).

The building was 6 Howard Street, and it typified Toronto's first, pre-World War I, apartment-house boom, especially concentrated along Jarvis, Sherbourne and nearby cross streets. Erected in 1914, and dubbed the 'Abernethy', it was one of the first blocks to require an exemption from the city's anti-apartment by-laws which prohibited such buildings from so-called 'residential' streets. It was a very respectable address, home to junior doctors, clerks and managers; but by the 1970s, buildings like the 'Abernethy' were nearing the ends of their lives, more like rooming houses than apartments. Shorn of its name and its verandas, the block was demolished after its roof collapsed in 2006, at the very least a case of 'demolition by neglect'.

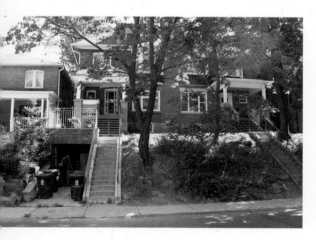

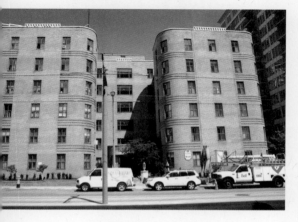

Above © Kevin Harrison
Opposite © Kevin Harrison

Similar buildings could be found in other eastern Canadian and American cities, but the point here is that it is possible to capture the spirit of Toronto by juxtaposing different forms of dwelling which, individually and architecturally, are not especially distinctive – a social *production* of space rather than just using location as a container for plot. This is evident in *Perfectly Normal* (Yves Simoneau, 1991), a mildly quirky comedy, in which the choices of domestic locations between them encapsulate a wide swathe of Toronto housing situations.

Renzo (Michael Riley), an Italian-Canadian brewery worker by day, cabdriver by night, occupies his late mother's apartment in the 'Fleetwood' on St Clair Avenue West. Six storeys, erected in 1939, and just along the street from the nine-storey Park Lane Apartments (1938) where the brilliant but eccentric pianist, Glenn Gould, made his home, the 'Fleetwood' epitomizes that once ritzy art deco elegance associated with Toronto's first love affair with apartment living before World War II. A step up from Miles's apartment in *Partner*, apartment houses like the 'Fleetwood', especially in middle-class neighbourhoods like Deer Park, were romantic but controversial interventions in the city's housing market, denigrated by opponents as un-British, anti-family and encouraging a lifestyle of bohemian immorality and irresponsibility. These notions were reinforced by the fact that they were invariably rented in a 'city of homes', a term which also implied homeownership, not tenancy. But they were also acknowledged to be useful housing for single career women and widows who wished to retain their independence. Renzo thus inherits his late mother's very respectable tenancy, qualified by their Italian ancestry, and unsurprisingly feels uncomfortable when confronted by the behaviour of his lodger, Alonzo Turner (Robbie Coltrane), who invites home glamorous women who may or may not be auditioning for parts in his proposed opera-restaurant. Intriguingly, the 'Fleetwood' also featured in David Cronenberg's *Videodrome* (1983), perhaps confirming its place outside conventional mores.

Renzo himself conforms to the Toronto ideal. He has purchased a 2-acre lot on the edge of the city where he plans to build his own home. In the course of the film, all that he completes is the timber 'balloon frame', which provides a surreal setting for private dinner parties with his girlfriend Denise (Deborah Duchene). The passion for self-building on Toronto's margins can be traced back to the beginning of the twentieth century in districts – such as Earlscourt (north of St Clair, west of Dufferin) – then, just outside city limits, and not subject to the central city's strict building regulations. Richard Harris calculated that, in the early years of the twentieth century, about a quarter of all new homes within the city, but 90 per cent beyond city limits, were owner-built. And the phenomenon is undergoing a new boom in the tough economic circumstances of the twenty-first century when many families cannot afford a conventional house erected by mainstream speculative builders.

Denise's own family home is conventional in its architecture but eccentric in its setting: it is set well back from the road but squeezed in between what look like walk-up apartment buildings, three storeys on one side, two storeys on the other, both covering the full depth of their plots. The ensemble is typical of the anarchic, unplanned inner suburbs originally developed during the 1930s and 1940s. Viewed from the street, Renzo's cab appears to overwhelm the tiny house. Denise is desperate to escape the moral as well as physical confines of this modest suburban environment.

Homes may be architecturally distinctive or they may be associated with particular lifestyles but, in combination, they powerfully signify Toronto. ✠

Similar buildings could be found in other eastern Canadian and American cities, but the point here is that it is possible to capture the spirit of Toronto by juxtaposing different forms of dwelling.

maps are only to be taken as approximates

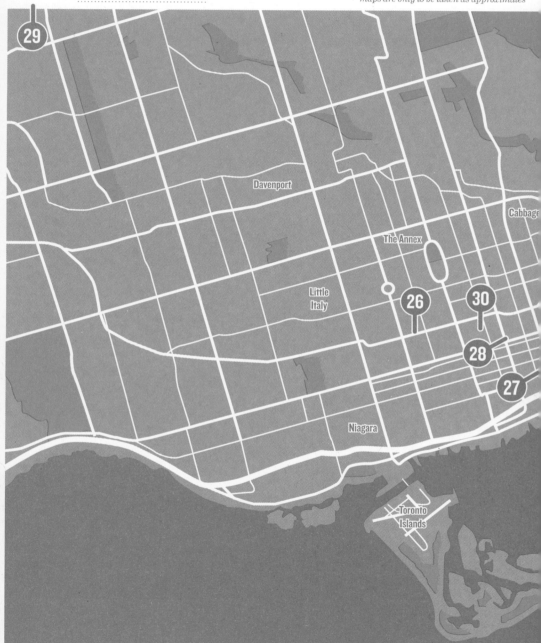

29

Davenport

Cabbage

The Annex

26

30

Little
Italy

28

27

Niagara

Toronto
Islands

TORONTO LOCATIONS
SCENES 25-30

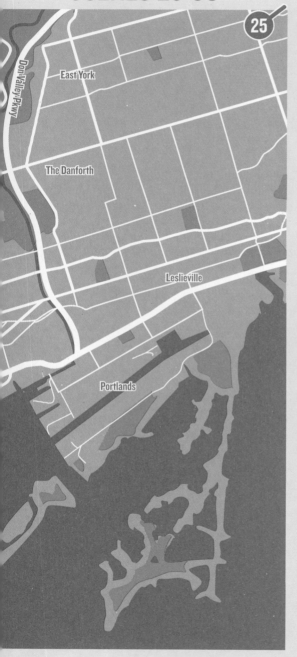

MY BIG FAT GREEK WEDDING (2002)

71 Glenwood Crescent, East York

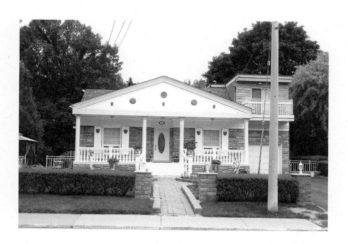

MY BIG FAT GREEK WEDDING explores Greek American culture, and is set in Chicago, where the film was partly shot. The film's central driving force, writer and leading actress, Nia Vardalos, was born in Winnipeg, Canada. The film-makers may have originally wanted Vardalos to change the ethnicity of her characters to Latino, and the promotional material may call it a 'US Hit'; but in filming Toronto's multi-national inhabitants alongside the leading actors, and using its Greektown as a primary shooting location, the film is infused with a personality that perfectly encapsulates the Greek Canadian strains in Vardalos's script. The Portokalos family household in *Greek Wedding* resides on a typical leafy street filled with middle-class suburban dwellings; however, their home looks like a replica of the Athenian Parthenon, replete with Ancient statues and a Greek flag garage door. The overbearing banner may be a fictional invention of the film's set designers, but the pseudo-classical home exists in reality next to Taylor Creek Park, near the Don River. In *Greek Wedding*, the overtly 'Greek' house exists to welcome 'native' loved ones, and signals to 'foreign' visitors where they are entering. This is most apparent in the scene when Ian Miller's parents visit. Confronted on the front lawn outside the house by a sizable Greek family roasting lamb on a spit, the Millers appear horrified, disdainful and confused as an awkward cultural exchange takes place. Their attitudes soften as the film progresses, but the distinctive East York house stands firm as a gateway to a different culture.
⊷ Carl Wilson

Directed by Joel Zwick
Scene description: The Miller family arrives at the Portokalos' home to be greeted by 'The Family'
and a culture that intimidates and terrifies them
Timecode for scene: 1:02:16 – 1:05:36

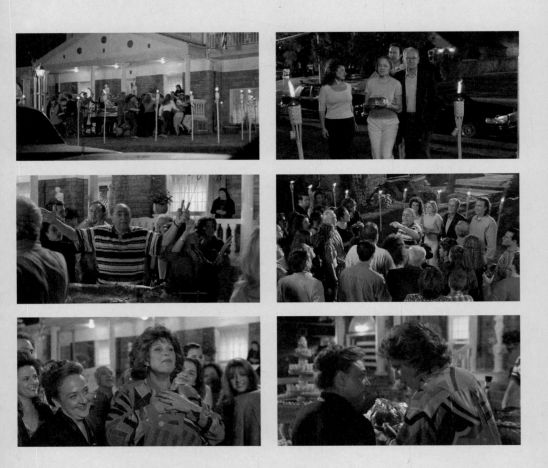

ARARAT (2002)

LOCATION *Art Gallery of Ontario, 317 Dundas Street West*

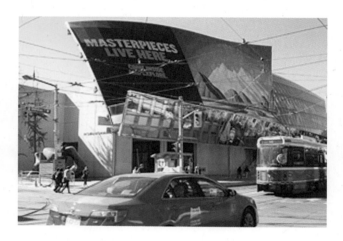

SOME OF THE FILM'S principal characters and storylines are juxtaposed in this scene where historian Ani (Arsinée Khanjian) lectures on the painter Arshile Gorky at the Art Gallery of Ontario. As she historicizes and gives a close reading of a 1912 photo of Gorky and his mother, the only one to exist of his early life, Ani's stepdaughter Celia (Marie-Josée Croze) interrupts with questions and challenges her. Director and writer Atom Egoyan melds together Ani's and Celia's personal family story with the larger historical one with which the film is preoccupied. He does so by incorporating, as audience members, director Edward Saroyan (Charles Aznavour) and screenwriter Rouben (Eric Bogosian), who aim to incorporate the historical Gorky into their film about the Armenian genocide. This scene is appropriately set in the Art Gallery of Ontario, one of North America's largest collections, and it brings together many kinds of art: the photo; Gorky's subsequent painting of it; Ani's book about him; Rouben's screenplay, which he has been researching on for five years; and Saroyan's film. A truly postmodern work, *Ararat* shows that the personal and social are inseparable and it articulates some of the ethical challenges of telling stories responsibly. It asks questions about how and why we narrate, and explores the boundaries between fiction and history.

⦁› Tom Ue

Photo © Tom Ue

Directed by Atom Egoyan
Scene description: Some of the film's principal characters are brought together in a lecture by Ani
Timecode for scene: 0:18:23 – 0:20:39

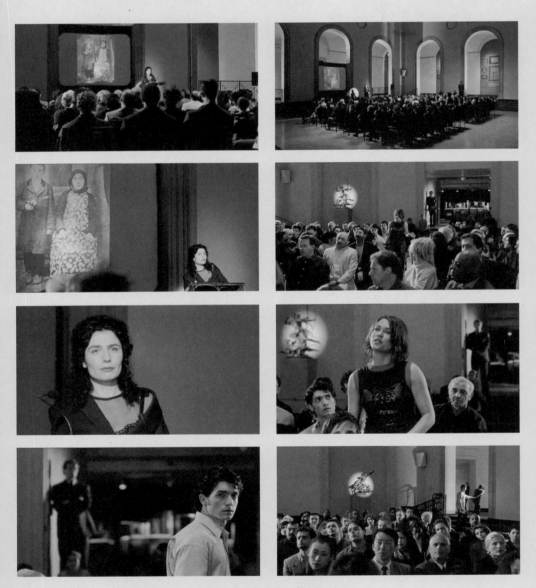

BOWLING FOR COLUMBINE (2002)

LOCATION *Crombie Park, 99 Scadding Avenue*

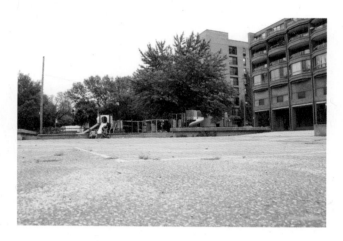

BOWLING FOR COLUMBINE blames gun culture and the media for the pervasive number of shooting deaths in America. Moore poses the question of why there are more instances of violence in the United States than there are in Canada. Dispelling some American-held myths by showing that Canadians indeed watch violent films, have a comparable unemployment rate, a diverse population and, surprisingly, own almost as many guns, he questions how such a dichotomy can exist between two nations that share the world's longest border. Moore further substantiates the contrast by noting the seriousness of Canadian news broadcasts, and the importance that they place on social programs and health care. His hunt for 'the indigent people' and the slums takes him to the Esplanade in the St Lawrence neighbourhood. The camera flashes over Crombie Park playground surrounded by well-kept homes. It is a peaceful, picturesque scene of kids playing baseball and a woman walking a dog, and he sums it up in voice-over: 'This is what a ghetto looks like in Canada.' While Toronto does have its share of poor, run-down areas, Moore has instead chosen a mixed income, ethnically diverse neighbourhood that neatly fits his hypothesis. It is a high-density area near the downtown core that sees luxury condos alongside subsidized housing and low-rent buildings. Safe and inviting, it is a paragon of inner-city community success that Moore can use as an ideal paradigm. In the end, *Bowling for Columbine* offers no answers, but the glaring mirror that Moore holds up to America compels us to keep questioning. **Fiona Luck**

Photo © Kevin Harrison

Directed by Michael Moore
Scene description: Michael Moore visits a 'ghetto' in Canada
Timecode for scene: 1:20:32 – 1:20:40

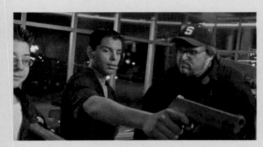 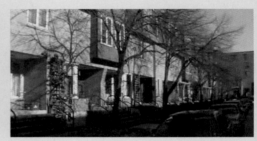

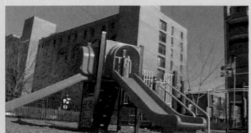 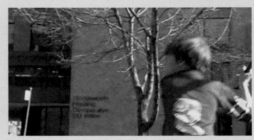

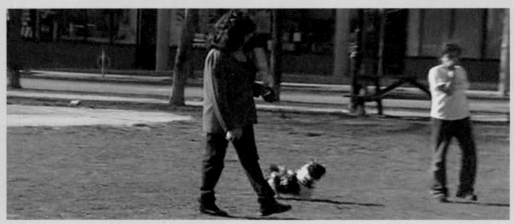

CHICAGO (2002)

LOCATION *The Elgin and Winter Garden Theatre Centre, 189 Yonge Street*

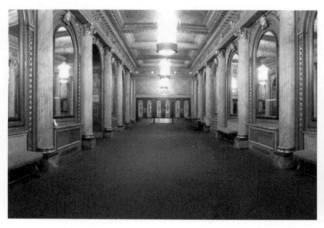
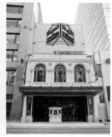

FOR A FILM FILLED with such quintessentially American themes (gangsters, Prohibition and the 'jazz age'), *Chicago* offers a rich visual inventory of staid Anglo-Canadian landmarks. Part of the film was shot at Casa Loma, the one-time mansion of Canadian financier Sir Henry Pellat, a location so English in spirit that it doubled as Hogwarts for the official launch of a Harry Potter film. Other vestiges of Old Toronto used in Chicago include the Elgin Theatre (built in 1913), Union Station (which opened in 1927) and Osgoode Hall, the nineteenth-century building which is still the centre of Ontario jurisprudence. The courtroom scene which serves as Chicago's climax was shot in Osgoode Hall, and features, as prosecuting attorney and judge, two Canadian actors who had each portrayed Canadian prime ministers in television mini-series – Colm Feore and Sean McCann, who had played Pierre Trudeau and Mackenzie King, respectively. The Ontario Legislative Building, which opened its doors in 1893, serves as the backdrop for the key press conference scene, in which accused murderer Roxie Hart (Renée Zellweger) and her attorney Billy Flynn (Richard Gere) face the Chicago media during the golden age of what historians now call 'jazz journalism'. The loosely Romanesque arches of the Legislative Building frame the film's main characters, while outside we see 1920s cars parked amidst snowdrifts. While the source materials behind Chicago have nourished some of the most American of Hollywood stories, it is difficult to think of another film which so relentlessly wears the trappings of Canadian institutional authority. ➠ *Will Straw*

Photos © Ontario Media Development Corporation

Directed by Rob Marshall
Scene description: 'Nowadays', the big wrap-up number in Chicago, filmed in Toronto's Elgin Theatre
Timecode for scene: 1:37:45 – 1:41:16

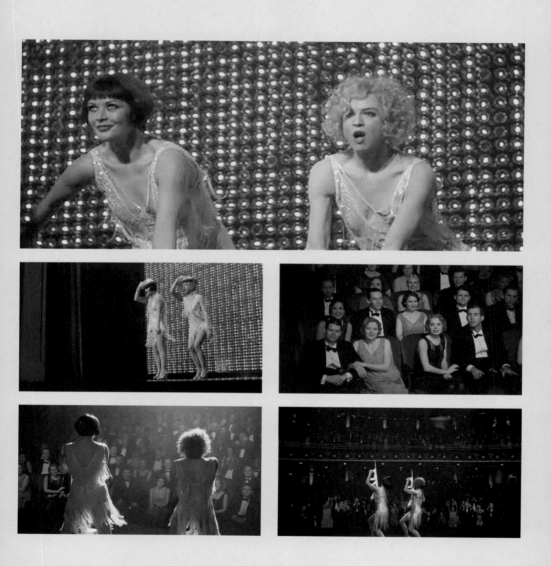

Images © 2002 Miramax Films/Producers Circle/Storyline Entertainment

THE PRINCE AND ME (2004)

LOCATION *The Underground Restaurant and Bar, York University Keele Campus*

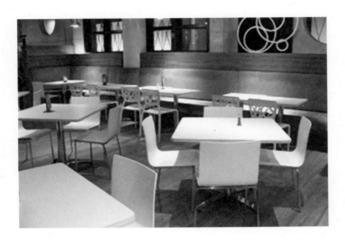

IN THE PRINCE AND ME, a young Danish prince (Luke Mably) attends a term of school at the University of Wisconsin, eager to discover the 'real' American college experience. The campus bar, Rathskeller, is where Eddie is convinced that he will find quintessential college life. Set in a true campus bar at Toronto's York University named The Underground, Eddie calls attention to the bar being located in a basement. Attempting to show off to bartender Paige (Julia Stiles), he says, 'You know, if we were in Germany right now, we'd be underground. Rathskeller – it means basement.' In fact, this basement is where Eddie is able to shed his identity as Crown Prince Edvard and assume his alias as Eddie Williams. Scenes in the bar signify that 'typical' American students include rowdy football fans, couples engaging in PDA, and friendly strangers with school spirit; these students provide for Eddie a novelty and reality previously unavailable. Under his new name, he realizes that, in a campus space, he is just another student and therefore must abide by common rules. He learns this when he upsets Paige, who hoses him down with soda, and when his parents refuse to fund his experiment in America and he must take a job at the bar. Eddie then experiences a descent in that he has truly gone underground – in name and in status – and takes on an inverted position: making sandwiches, cleaning out garbage, hosing down tarmacs and cleaning the kitchen on his knees. Finally, he falls in love with the self-proclaimed farm girl Paige, for whom such tasks are an honest way to pay for one's way through school. **⊷Lai-Tze Fan**

Photo © Lai-Tze Fan

Directed by Martha Coolidge
Scene description: Eddie visits the campus bar for the first time
Timecode for scene: 0:17:58 – 0:21:07

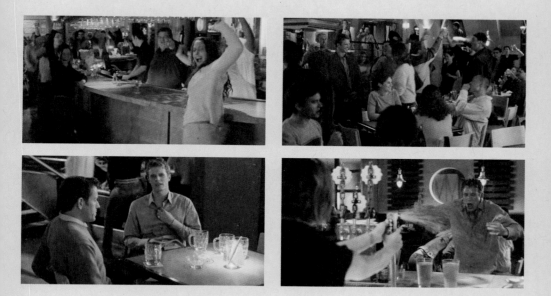

RESIDENT EVIL: APOCALYPSE (2004)

LOCATION *Nathan Phillips Square, 100 Queen Street West*

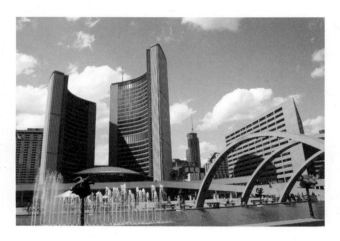

ALICE'S (MILLA JOVOVICH) ESCAPE from the plagued Raccoon City of Alexander Witt's *Resident Evil: Apocalypse* showcases a barely disguised downtown Toronto transformed into a dark, sinister, zombie-infested prison, wherein even the CN Tower makes a rare and cheeky appearance. To contain the virus, the remaining humans are barred from leaving the city at Raven's Gate, which is, in reality, the Prince Edward Viaduct. Its own Luminous Veil suicide barrier is used to great effect. The viaduct looms over the panicked mob and, ironically, cages them in to certain doom: the Veil was actually installed in 2003 to save lives by thwarting would be jumpers. This confining function is most apparent at the climactic battle between Alice and Nemesis (Matthew G. Taylor) at the Nathan Phillips Square. Its inward curving towers frame the scene, operating as a colosseum-like arena around Alice's fight to the death. When Alice runs down the length of Toronto's City Hall, physical aspects of her character are translated into the setting. Alice is formidable and strong, yet beautiful and feminine. The building too has an imposing and unyielding presence, yet remains graceful and elegant. The two towers and its saucer-like council chamber have a perpetually futuristic feel though they were built in the early 1960s: they even earned a cameo appearance in *Star Trek: The Next Generation* (Gene Roddenberry, CBS, 1987–98). Flanked by a Peace Garden and a picturesque reflecting pool dedicated to freedom, the square is an unlikely place for a mutant battle, but indeed hoards of the undead converge upon its doorstep. **➥Fiona Luck**

Photo © Kevin Harrison

Directed by Alexander Witt
Scene description: *Alice battles Nemesis to save her friends and escape a town filled with zombies*
Timecode for scene: *1:07:14 – 1:10:14*

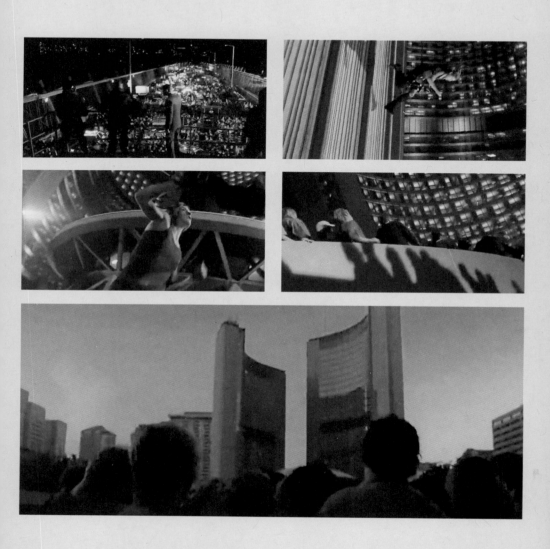

EVERYWHERE AND NOWHERE

David Cronenberg's Toronto

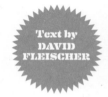
Text by
DAVID
FLEISCHER

THE KNOCK AGAINST David Cronenberg has always been that his films have a tendency towards being cold or antiseptic – okay, that and they can be a bit icky for the average filmgoer. Over the past few years, he has expanded his geographical palette, shooting *A Dangerous Method* (2001) in Germany and *Eastern Promises* (2007) in London, but Toronto has always been his hometown and his home base. Stereotypically, Toronto has faced some of the same criticisms as Cronenberg's films. As Marge Simpson wryly noted when her family visited, 'It's so clean and bland. I'm home!' evoking qualities often lobbed both at the city and Cronenberg's films. At times, he has worked around Toronto's apparent lack of place, using the city to play New York in *Cosmopolis* (2012) and the even more exotic Interzone for *Naked Lunch* (1991). But in other instances, he has taken full advantage of Toronto's blank slate, setting films

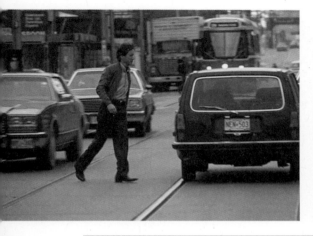

in the city while simultaneously revelling in the anonymity that it provides.

In *The Fly* (1986), he shows a grimier side of the city. Though it has since been cleaned up, somewhat like New York's Times Square, we see Seth Brundle (Jeff Goldblum) strolling past the pawn shops and strip clubs of the Yonge–Dundas area downtown. Speaking of gentrification, Goldbum's laboratory is located amidst the anonymous brick warehouses of Liberty Village. A quarter-century later, however, the area has become filled with lofts, clubs and other hipster haunts. The exterior of Manulife Insurance's office, near Bloor and Yonge Streets, stands in for the publishing company at which Veronica Quaife (Geena Davis) works ('Monolith Publishing', naturally). It is a unique structure with a glossy 1980s-style facade, but also a cupola-topped entrance that makes it seem like a strange, corporate church. The interiors, however, were shot at an office tower at Yonge and Front Streets, presenting a view of Toronto's landmark Flatiron Building and its distinctive *trompe l'œil*. Films that shoot Toronto as elsewhere usually avoid its most obvious landmarks, like the CN Tower. *The Fly* makes no comment on the city in which it takes place, but Cronenberg tips his hand late in the movie, when Quaife visits Toronto General Hospital and the tower's distinctive spike is clearly visible in the background.

Whereas *The Fly* at least gets out and about in Toronto, the city presented in *Crash* (1996) takes its anonymity to the extreme as Cronenberg turns its on-ramps and streets into sexually charged settings. James Ballard (James Spader) and Catherine Ballard (Deborah Kara Unger)

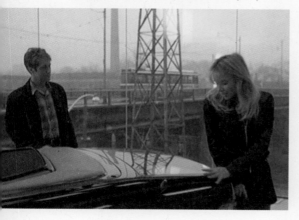

live in an apartment on Graydon Hall Drive that overlooks a major cloverleaf. This is the intersection of Highway 401 and the Don Valley Parkway (DVP), two of the busiest highways in the region. Seduction scenes take place in the most unlikely locations. One is a Mercedes dealership perched over the DVP at Queen Street. (Amusingly, the same dealership hosted an Aretha Franklin number in *Blues Brothers 2000* [John Landis, 1998], which tried to portray Toronto as Chicago.) A number of crucial scenes, including a vicious accident, take place on the highway itself, just below. Ballard and Helen Remington (Holly Hunter) also enjoy each other's company in parking lots at Harbourfront, abutting the Gardiner Expressway, and a now-demolished lot at Toronto's Pearson Airport. One rare, distinctive local landmark is the old Joy Gas Station at Lakeshore Boulevard and Windemere Avenue. More than a dozen of the castle-like stations once dotted the Toronto landscape. This was the last of the dying breed, since restored and relocated across the street.

Videodrome (1983) and *Dead Ringers* (1988) are probably Cronenberg's most explicitly Toronto films, something best appreciated if you live in the city. In the former, Max Renn's (James Woods) employer, Civic TV, is overtly modelled on Toronto's CityTV, particularly its one-time claim to fame, airing soft-porn movies at night. CityTV is still on

Stereotypically, Toronto has faced some of the same criticisms as Cronenberg's films. As Marge Simpson wryly noted when her family visited, 'It's so clean and bland. I'm home!'

the air, but now corporate owned and porn-free. In some of the shots of Civic TV's exterior, one can see a few of Toronto's bank towers, but the actual filming location on Wellington Street seems to have been absorbed by the development of the Brookfield Place. (The closest that one can come to the location is by visiting the stunning Brookfield atrium, in which some of the historic streetscape is preserved.) One of the film's most crucial settings is the seedy Cathode Ray Mission. Until shortly after the production wrapped, the building at the corner of Bathurst and Adelaide Streets has become home to Toronto's independent Factory Theatre. Additionally, various analyses have suggested that the Brian O'Blivion's character (Jack Creley) pays homage to Torontonians like Marshall McLuhan (best known for coining, 'The medium is the message' [McLuhan and Fiore, p. 9, 26]) and Moses Znaimer, CityTV's innovative founder.

Plotwise, *Dead Ringers* could take place anywhere but a title at the start explicitly identifies Toronto as the location. That said, Cronenberg rarely shoots locations as they are. The Conservatory at Casa Loma (also seen in films ranging from *X-Men* [Bryan Singer, 2000] to *The Love Guru* [Marco Schnabel, 2008]) plays a fancy restaurant and suburban Mississauga's then-new City Hall doubles as a banquet hall and a lecture hall. The easiest Toronto landmark to spot, though the surroundings have since changed, is the church outside the apartment in which Beverly Mantle (Jeremy Irons) lives. It is the Church of the Holy Trinity, just outside the Toronto Eaton Centre and, incidentally, where the Cowboy Junkies recorded their seminal album, *The Trinity Session* (1988).

The idea that even the most innocuous community has a seamy underside predates the likes of *Blue Velvet* (David Lynch, 1986) and *Peyton Place* (Mark Robson, 1957), but Toronto has rarely been explored in this context. There is a perverse joy in the notion that creepy gynaecological practices, compromised scientific experiments and even the fetishization of traffic infrastructure might all be taking place beneath the veneer of a city colloquially known, for its bland Protestant past, as 'Toronto the Good'. Certainly, no one would mistake Cronenberg's Toronto for, say, Woody Allen's postcard New York. It would perhaps be easy to say that many of Cronenberg's films do not have a particular, specific sense of place, but that would be missing the point. Toronto is a blank slate. Toronto *is* the place. ✤

LOCATIONS MAP

TORONTO

maps are only to be taken as approximates

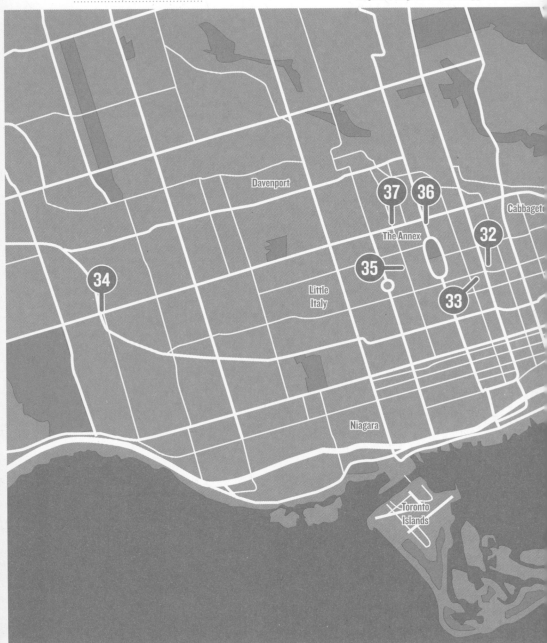

Davenport

37 36

Cabbaget

The Annex

32

34

35

Little
Italy

33

Niagara

Toronto
Islands

TORONTO LOCATIONS
SCENES 31-37

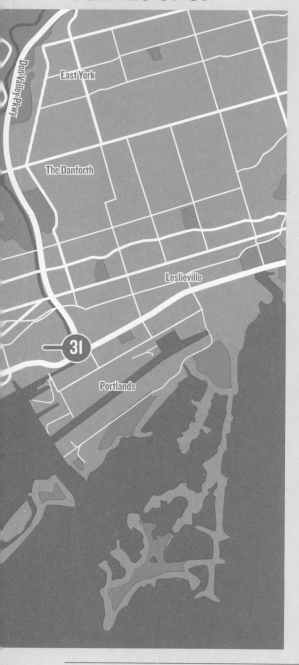

ASSAULT ON PRECINCT 13 (2005)

LOCATION *CN Rail Police Building, 453 Cherry Street, West Don Lands*

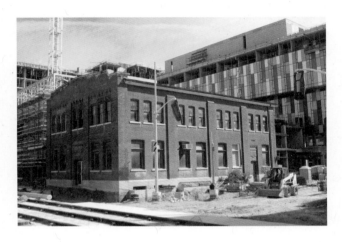

ASSAULT ON PRECINCT 13 is an update of John Carpenter's gritty 1976 remake of the 1959 classic western *Rio Bravo* (Howard Hawks). In all three films, a notorious criminal, temporarily incarcerated in an ill-equipped police station, has to be protected by a few beleaguered lawmen and dysfunctional volunteers against a faceless mob. The setting, therefore, is absolutely critical as both a literal and metaphoric last-bastion of law, order and humanity. Carpenter's *Assault on Precinct 13* used a real Los Angeles police station as its central location, and this contributed to the film an increased degree of authenticity. The 2005 version adopts this logic by using an old red-brick railway police building that was constructed in Toronto's West Don Lands in the early 1920s. Now owned by the government, this building has been used as a shooting location for numerous films, including *Frequency* (Gregory Hoblit, 2000). The classically inspired office building looks uniquely imposing in the environment. However, several adjustments have been made to the actual Toronto location in Richet's reincarnation – specifically in the scene where the camera dollies back from Sgt Jack Roenick (Ethan Hawke), sitting emotionally scarred and alone in his office, through the barred windows, and cranes up to show the building in total isolation. Richet has added an entirely new construction onto the side of the building, and has sprinkled so many CGI power lines, roads and distant buildings around it that, while the story claims to be set in Detroit, Toronto has vanished almost entirely underneath the computer-generated snowstorm. **↝Carl Wilson**

Photo © Kevin Harrison

Directed by Jean-François Richet
Scene description: Sgt Jake Roenick sits in his office and reads
a psychiatrist's medical report about himself
Timecode for scene: 0:20:14 – 0:20:47

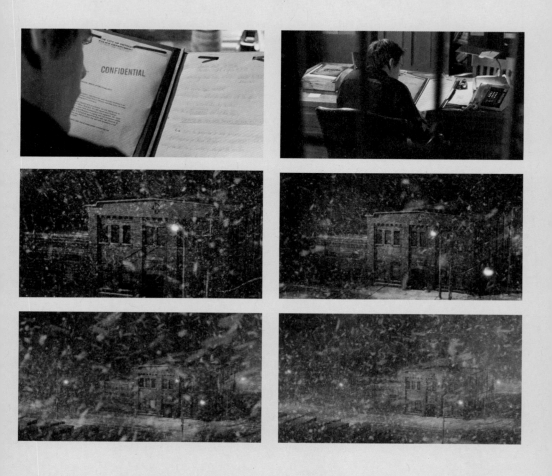

CINDERELLA MAN (2005)

LOCATION *Carlu (College Park) Banquet Gall, 444 Yonge Street*

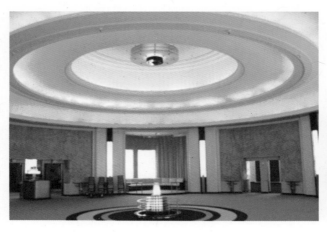

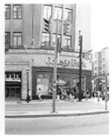

IN *CINDERELLA MAN*, down-and-out boxer Jim Braddock (Russell Crowe) spends most of his time around Depression-era New York in crowded tenements, smoky rooms and dark arenas. One notable exception is the black-tie event at which he runs into rival Max Baer (Craig Bierko). The room's perfect Art Moderne stylings are likely supposed to represent Rockefeller Centre's storied Rainbow Room, but it is actually Toronto's Carlu banquet hall, located at Yonge and College Streets. Work started on the flagship of the Eaton's department-store chain in 1928, but plans for a 38-storey skyscraper were curtailed with the onset of the Depression, leading to the shorter (but still impressive) structure there today. The top may have been lopped off but no expense was spared on the interiors of the building known today as College Park. Jacques Carlu was brought in to design the seventh floor, including a concert hall that would host the likes of Glenn Gould. The Round Room, with its Lalique fountain, seen here, became the prototype for the Rainbow Room, which opened in 1934. Amazingly, perhaps the most impressive piece of the city's architecture from that era was shuttered in 1977. It was neglected and might have even been demolished if it was not designated a national historic site. New owners restored and reopened it as a banquet facility, just in time for Hollywood to come calling. **⤏David Fleischer**

Directed by Ron Howard
Scene description: Jim Braddock attends a fancy party before his fight with Max Baer
Timecode for scene: 1:36:18 – 1:40:42

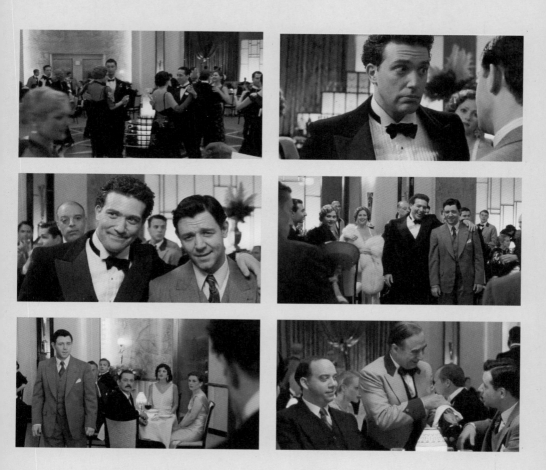

A HISTORY OF VIOLENCE (2005)

LOCATION *Stoopy's Tavern, 376 Dundas Street East*

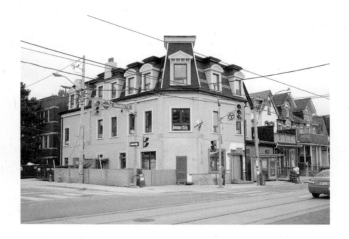

IT MIGHT STRIKE SOME as ironic that this American pastoral of regeneration through violence was shot entirely on Canadian soil. But David Cronenberg's cinematic misdirections are right at home in a film whose protagonist, Tom Stall (Viggo Mortensen), has trapped himself in a decades-long performance of a wholesome American family man. Both Stall and Cronenberg are myth-makers; they saturate their respective worlds with iconic images of American innocence and prosperity in order to deceive sceptical onlookers. Take this sequence at the Track and Turf bar as an example. The scene was shot in Stoopy's Tavern, a defunct bar in the residential neighbourhood of Moss Park. Cronenberg leverages iconic American mise-en-scène to transform this Canadian space into an urban dive bar in Philadelphia, the historic metropolis of the United States. Stall exits his beat-up pickup truck in cowboy boots and rugged jeans. He enters the bar, flanked on all sides by neon signs and beer advertisements, including several for Yuengling, a Philadelphia staple and America's oldest brewing company. Stall's drink purchase takes on an air of ritual as Cronenberg's camera lingers on the transaction, insisting on the American dollars as they change hands. When he sits down across from the greasy mobster Ruben (Ian Matthews), Stall's face is half-shrouded in shadow, and the viewers are finally confronted with the incredible depth of his deception. His frozen smile slides away and is replaced by the placid, eerie visage of another man entirely. 'You Joey?' Ruben asks, and the man we thought was named Tom Stall replies: 'Yeah, I'm Joey.'
⇢Corey Waite Arnold

Photo © Kevin Harrison

Scene description: Tom Stall returns to Philadelphia to face his past
Timecode for scene: 1:12:56 – 1:15:07

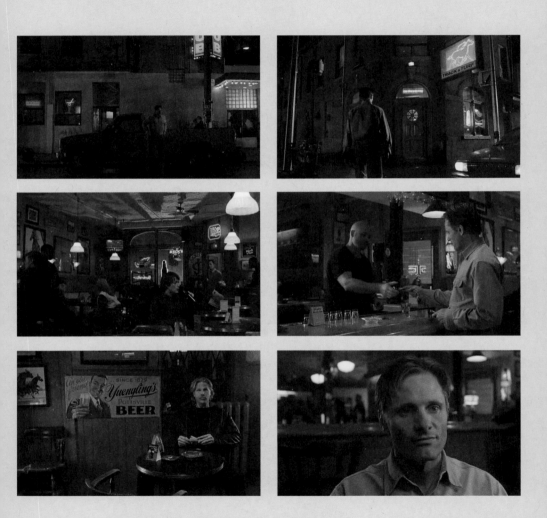

HAIRSPRAY (2007)

LOCATION *Starbucks Coffee, corner of Dundas and Roncesvalles Streets*

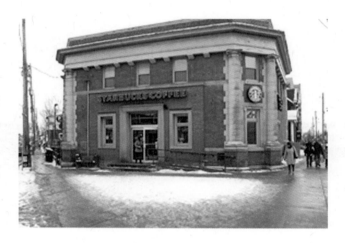

THAT CANADIAN CITIES regularly stand in for American locations in Hollywood films is well known. Vancouver, with its mountains still visible, famously tried to pass undetected as the Bronx in the Jackie Chan vehicle *Rumble in the Bronx* (Stanley Tong, 1995). Hollywood production companies shoot in Canada because of tax breaks and lower labour costs, but they are motivated, as well, by the perception that Canadian cities look the way US cities looked several decades ago. *Hairspray*, the 2007 adaptation of the Broadway musical based on John Waters's 1988 film of the same name, is set in early-1960s Baltimore, and no place seems to look more like 1960s Baltimore than Toronto's west end. Even today, Roncesvalles Street bustles with the busy commerce of a post-World War II working-class neighbourhood and Dundas Street, which it crosses, is dotted with the faded signage and residual businesses (like men's barber shops) of the 1950s or 1960s. At the corner where these two streets meet, aspiring performer Tracy Turnblad (Nikki Blonsky) and her house-bound mother (John Travolta) go to Mr Pinky's Hefty Hideaway, a store catering to full-figured women. When *Hairspray* was being shot in Toronto, the building dressed up as Hefty Hideway was still a bank – famous, the 'Lost Toronto' blog tells us, as the first bank to be robbed by Toronto's notorious 'Boyd Gang', in 1951. By 2010, the building housed a Starbucks Coffee, one more sign of the gentrification creeping across this most interesting of neighbourhoods. **↝ Will Straw**

Photo © Will Straw

Directed by Adam Shankman
Scene description: An exterior view of Mr Pinky's Hefty Hideaway
Timecode for scene: 0:39:41 – 0:43:22

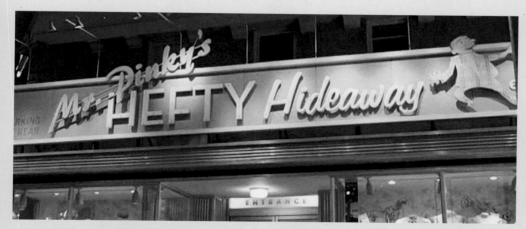

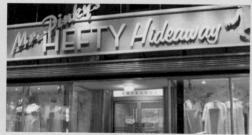

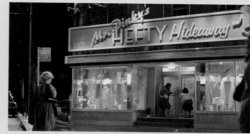

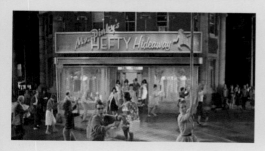

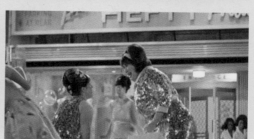

THE INCREDIBLE HULK (2008)

Knox College, 59 St George Street

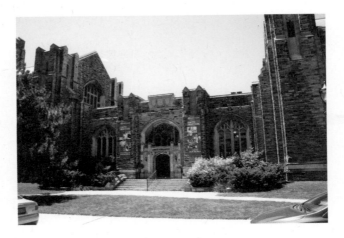

SERVING AS BOTH reboot and sequel to the earlier *Hulk* (Ang Lee, 2003) film, *The Incredible Hulk* follows scientist Bruce Banner's (Edward Norton) odyssey to cure himself of the gamma radiation that transforms him into a gigantic, super-strong, super-angry green behemoth. Whereas the 2003 *Hulk* film was situated at the real-life campus of the University of California, Berkeley, this time Banner finds his way to the fictional campus of Culver University. (The name 'Culver' is a nod to the *Incredible Hulk* television series from 1978–82, in which Banner [Bill Bixby] worked at the Culver Institute.) After a brief reunion, Betty Ross (Liv Tyler) can only look on while General 'Thunderbolt' Ross (William Hurt) and Emil Blonsky (Tim Roth) lead heavily armed soldiers and tanks across campus to capture Banner. Visible during the chaos are several University of Toronto buildings: University College, Convocation Hall and the Sir Daniel Wilson Hall. The cross-campus pursuit ends at a glass corridor; and surrounded on both sides, Banner is forced to transform into the Hulk behind a thick shroud of teargas. A full-blown battle then erupts in the middle of the campus quad between the enraged Hulk, tanks, soldiers and supersonic gunships. The special effects-heavy showdown was filmed right at the doorstep of University of Toronto's Knox College. The carnage of the Hulk scenes may seem at odds with the college's quiet and peaceful demeanour. Founded in 1844, Knox College is known for its distinctive perpendicular neo-Gothic style of architecture and stony grey facades that serve as home to its ministry and theology students. ⁍ *Tyler Shores*

Photo © Kevin Harrison

Directed by Louis Leterrier
Scene description: Bruce Banner is chased across the fictional campus
of Culver University before he transforms into the Incredible Hulk
Timecode for scene: 0:47:58 – 0:58:10

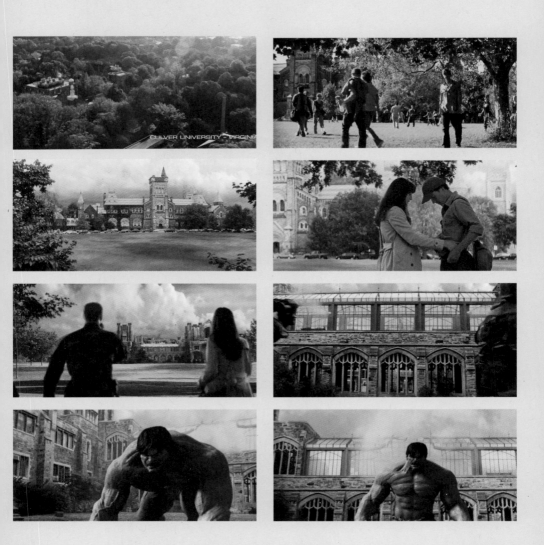

TORONTO STORIES (2008)

LOCATION *Royal Ontario Museum, 100 Queens Park*

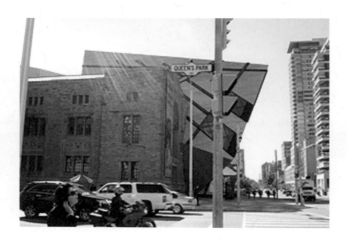

A COLLABORATIVE EFFORT, *Toronto Stories* presents the city as cultivated and multicultural. Beginning with a boy (Toka Murphy) who arrives at Pearson International Airport without any identification, the film brings together four interconnected stories. The diverse range of characters engages with Toronto as a space of quiet residence, lively urbanity, sequestering for the homeless and, above all, as a space of exploration of their relationships. In the story 'The Brazilian', Willia (Sook-Yin Lee) develops feelings for Boris (Tygh Runyan), despite his poor social skills, idealizations of love and lack of romantic interest in her. In an attempt to form a relationship, they plan a date at Toronto's Royal Ontario Museum (commonly referred to as the 'ROM'). Outside of The Crystal main entrance, which was built in 2007 to replace a previous one, Willia waits for Boris. As the pair fails to maintain eye contact or conversation, they turn their attention towards the exhibits, visiting the Gallery of Birds and a display of endangered reptiles at the Schad Gallery of Biodiversity. At the Prince Takamodo Gallery of Japan, Willia imagines the trials of samurai battle and Boris, a self-proclaimed 'builder of things', curtails the conversation by noting the armour's lack of practicality. Later in the ROM's interactive autumnal wood, Willia offers Boris belated birthday presents. As he inquires into her design plan of the homemade card, the two keep a safe distance on a park bench, a soundtrack of chirping birds in the background. ↝*Lai-Tze Fan*

Photo © Tom Ue

Directed by Sook-Yin Lee, Sudz Sutherland, David Weaver, Aaron Woodley
Scene description: Willia and Boris visit the Royal Ontario Museum for a date
Timecode for scene: 0:32:23 – 0:34:55

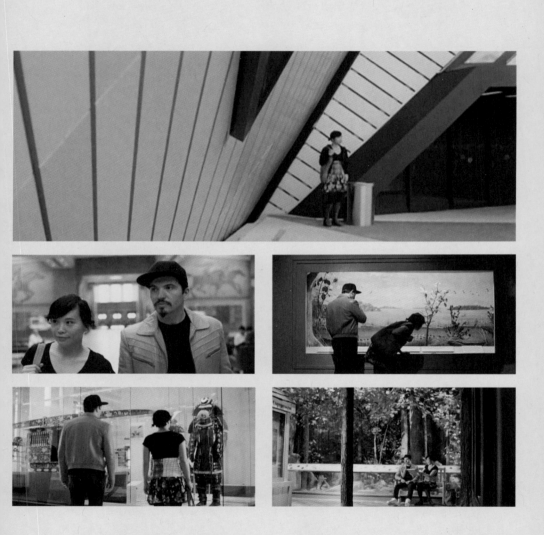

CHLOE (2009)

Mazzoleni Concert Hall (in Ihnatowycz Hall), The Royal Conservatory of Music, 273 Bloor Street West

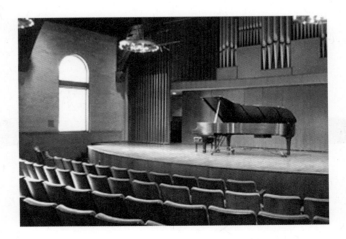

ALTHOUGH FILMED in several Toronto locations, Atom Egoyan's *Chloe* is distinctive for opting to use the Mazzoleni Concert Hall. A part of The Royal Conservatory of Music's heritage building, Ihnatowycz Hall, the Mazzoleni is an intimate, 237-seat theatre with Romanesque revival-style arched doorways, low-hanging lights and an exposed stone and wood interior. Originally belonging to McMaster Baptist College, Ihnatowycz Hall, formerly known as the McMaster Hall, was built in 1881, and the Mazzoleni Concert Hall, previously the Castle Memorial Hall, in 1901. In 1963, they became home to The Royal Conservatory of Music. Renovated in 1997, the space juxtaposes old and new, making it an apt location for Egoyan to situate Catherine Stewart (Julianne Moore) on evenings out with her husband David (Liam Neeson) and son (Max Thieriot) directly after her two most character-altering moments. The concert that the family attends, to which Neeson's character arrives late, occurs directly after Catherine sees a picture of him embracing his student (Meghan Heffern), which she construes as evidence of infidelity. The later scene depicts her son's piano recital, at which she does not sit beside her husband. Both scenes offer a glimpse of nearby Royal Ontario Museum, the first through the Mazzoleni's window, the second, as Catherine walks away from her son's concert. This second scene immediately follows Catherine and Chloe's (Amanda Seyfried) first kiss, which arises from Chloe's account of her hotel tryst with David. The Concert Hall offers a backdrop for Catherine's shifting relationships, first with David, then with Chloe. **➻Sheri Chriqui**

Photo © Tom Ue

Directed by Atom Egoyan
Scene description: The Stewarts attend their son's piano recital
Timecode for scene: 0:54:38 – 0:55:59

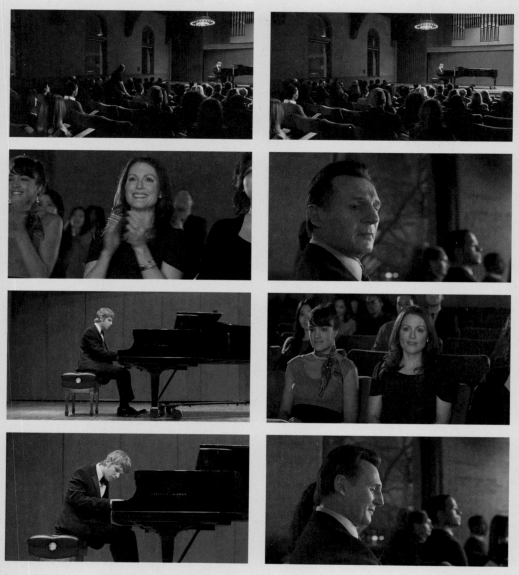

THE ANONYMOUS METROPOLIS

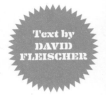
Text by
DAVID
FLEISCHER

It is a great trope of the superhero genre that most heroes ply their trade in anonymous-but-familiar cities like Metropolis and Gotham – New York resident Spider-Man being a notable exception. In that context, it is a bit surprising that Toronto, the generic modern city par excellence, has not been the go-to place for large-scale superhero flicks. The Marvel renaissance of the past few years touched down in the form of *The Incredible Hulk* (Louis Leterrier, 2008) but comic blockbusters have largely looked elsewhere. *The Avengers* (Joss Whedon, 2012) mixed New York and Cleveland footage, for example, while Christopher Nolan used a mishmash of Pittsburgh, Chicago, New York, London, Los Angeles, and some special effects to

create Gotham City for his Batman trilogy.

Yet, it is somehow perfect that Toronto would provide a home for *Kick-Ass* (Matthew Vaughn, 2010), which both skewers and pays tribute to its forebears. *Kick-Ass* is set in the not-quite-New York that Toronto excels at playing. The opening shot, for example, takes place atop an anonymous skyscraper, from which the Empire State Building is unmistakably visible. But the angular golden facade of the building from which the costumed not-hero is about to jump is recognizable to any Torontonian as the headquarters of the Royal Bank of Canada.

As the unnamed character leaps to his death (being bereft of the power of flight) we see onlookers watching from Bay Street, the heart of Toronto's financial district, culminating in the un-super-powered individual crashing into a car below.

Indeed, the entire film was shot in London and Toronto, with a few half-hearted background shots of the Big Apple itself thrown in. In one scene, for example, Hit Girl (Chloë Grace Moretz) and Kick-Ass (Aaron Taylor-Johnson) cruise through what's supposed to be Times Square. The commercial district in the Yonge–Dundas area often passes for Times Square in New York-set movies, but rarely passes muster if you're really paying attention. The pair cruise past Toronto landmarks like the Toronto Eaton Centre and Sam the Record Man, a music store that has since been shuttered and demolished.

Before a Kick-Ass impersonator gets unceremoniously (and mistakenly) killed, we see one of the ubiquitous Tim Hortons coffee shops

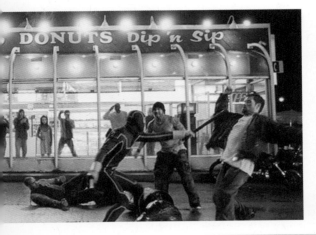

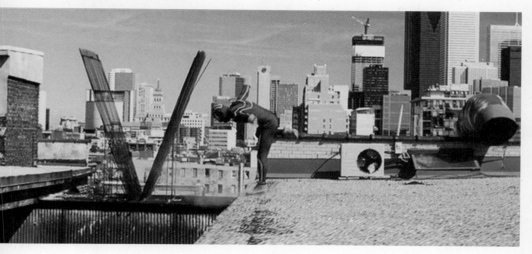

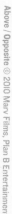

that dot the Greater Toronto area – this one is on Richmond Street, near University Avenue – and thus the city does not exactly shout 'New York'. This becomes more prominent in other scenes, as in the one in which Kick-Ass practices jumping off a building's rooftop, Toronto's distinctively un-Manhattan skyline clearly visible in the background. Similarly, a finale in which the hero flies around New York in a jetpack, includes a flight down Toronto's University Avenue, a Broadway-style boulevard, in the middle of which sits the Ontario Legislative Building, a great limestone edifice which looks totally unlike anything to be seen in New York City.

One can also see the skyline a bit when Red Mist (Christopher Mintz-Plasse) takes Kick-Ass to an ambush in an old industrial district. The location, at the east end of Front Street, has served the same purpose in other films, perhaps most notably in the finale of *Scott Pilgrim vs. The World* (Edgar Wright, 2010). That movie ends with a virtually identical shot looking back towards the towers of the financial district but *Kick-Ass* makes sure to frame out the CN Tower – always a dead giveaway that you are not in New York City.

Toronto seems to have fewer dingy alleyways which is, perhaps, why the same alley on Queen Street West, near Bathurst, seems to get used by Hollywood productions constantly. Here it provides the setting for a meeting between Kick-Ass and his would-be nemesis, Red Mist. In the past it has hosted the likes of Steven Segal and Chuck Norris, causing director Edgar Wright to suggest half-jokingly that it should have a plaque commemorating its cinematic heritage. His *Scott Pilgrim*, also a postmodern superhero film of sorts, used the alley for a confrontation with one-time Superman, Brandon Routh. Because of the logistics, however, a photo of the actual alley was used as a green-screen background and the rest built as a soundstage set. Fans will have to travel a bit further afield to visit some of the other locations. Key scenes at a high school where a nascent Kick-Ass is beaten by thugs were filmed about an hour away in Hamilton. Kick-Ass's first triumph, outside an old-style donut shop, was filmed at the Dip'n Sip on 663 Kingston Road, Upper Beaches.

The team came back to the city (with Toronto native Jim Carrey onboard) to shoot the less-impressive *Kick-Ass 2* (2013) in mid-2012. They returned to old haunts like the ersatz Times Square area at Yonge and Dundas and ventured out into suburban Mississauga for a big (and gruesome) confrontation with the police. The quality drop-off in a sequel may be par for the course but at least it seems that the city is doing a good job playing up its not-quite-New-York-ness. Superman and Batman are off fighting crime elsewhere, but Toronto may finally have found a hero of its own. ✦

The quality drop-off in a sequel may be par for the course but at least it seems that the city is doing a good job playing up its not-quite-New-York-ness. Superman and Batman are off fighting crime elsewhere, but Toronto may finally have found a hero of its own.

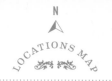

TORONTO

maps are only to be taken as approximates

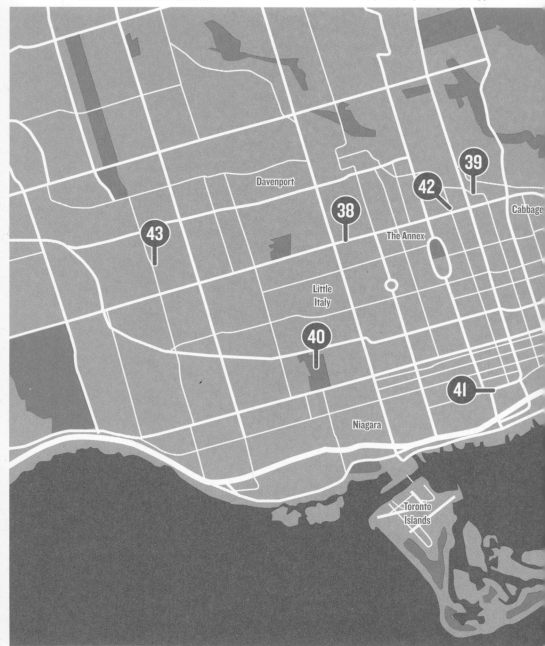

Davenport

Cabbage

The Annex

Little Italy

Niagara

Toronto Islands

39

42

38

43

40

41

TORONTO LOCATIONS
SCENES 38-44

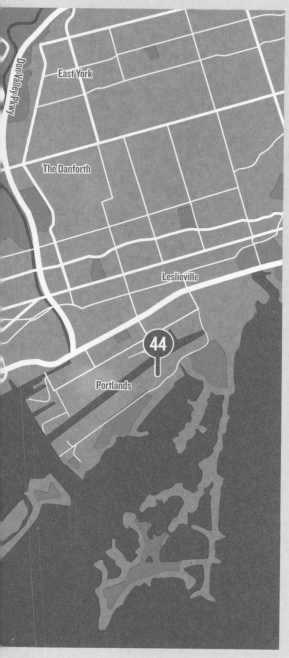

SCOTT PILGRIM VS. THE WORLD (2010)

Lee's Palace, 529 Bloor Street West

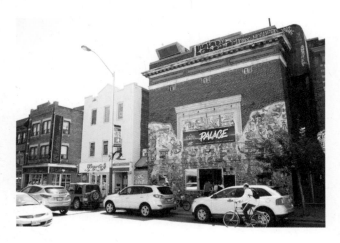

THE OPENING SCROLL, 'Not so long ago ... in the mysterious land ... of Toronto, Canada ...' introduces audiences into the filmic universe of *Scott Pilgrim vs. the World*. Filmed entirely in Toronto, the big-screen adaptation of the six-volume *Scott Pilgrim* graphic novel series combines a decidedly video game-inspired aesthetic with a very particular level of local realism. As director Edgar Wright noted: '[I]f we hadn't shot in Toronto, as far as I'm concerned, the film wouldn't have happened at all' (quoted by Mudhar). That commitment to verisimilitude makes Lee's Palace, the uber-popular alternative music venue, a natural setting for many of the film's key scenes. When Scott Pilgrim (Canadian Michael Cera) and his band Sex Bob-omb arrive at Lee's for the Toronto International Battle of the Bands, they encounter a rival band that just happens to be fronted by Scott's ex-girlfriend Envy Adams (Brie Larson), and Todd Ingram (Brandon Routh), the Third Evil Ex. Some interiors were shot thanks to a reconstruction of the venue prior to its 2005 renovations. Sharp-eyed fans might also notice that Scott Pilgrim creator Bryan Lee O'Malley makes an un-credited appearance as a Lee's Palace bar patron, right in the corner from where Scott and friends are shown to hang out. Located in downtown Toronto's Annex neighbourhood, the two-floor building dates back over a century, with the one-time movie theatre converted into its modern-day incarnation in 1985. Today, the top floor functions as the hipster club known as The Dance Cave, with the bottom floor serving as one of the city's most important music hotspots. Lee's Palace has been home to many headlining acts, and, to answer Scott's blithely meta-textual question ('They make movies in Toronto?'), even the occasional film setting. ↪**Tyler Shores**

Photo © Kevin Harrison

Directed by Edgar Wright
Scene description: Scott Pilgrim and his band Sex Bob-omb encounter
a rival band and Scott discovers the Third Evil Ex
Timecode for scene: 1:00:25 – 1:02:43

NOT SO LONG AGO...
IN THE MYSTERIOUS LAND...
OF TORONTO, CANADA...

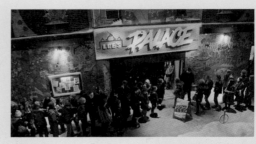

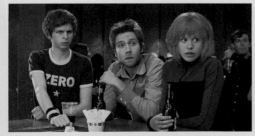

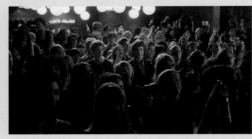

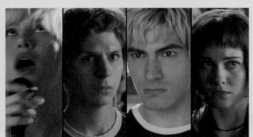

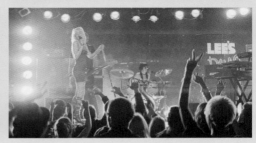

Images © 2010 Big Talk Productions/Marc Platt Productions/Universal Pictures

RED (2010)

Toronto Reference Library, 789 Yonge Street

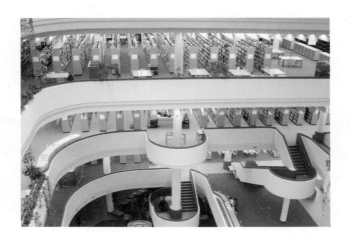

FRANK MOSES (BRUCE WILLIS) is a former CIA agent who is trying to settle down and enjoy his retirement. Lonely and bored, he makes excuses to call his pension office and awkwardly flirt with a customer service rep named Sarah (Mary-Louise Parker) with whom he has never met but on whom he clearly has a crush. After a hit squad tries to kill him, Frank must go on the run and search for answers. Knowing that his phone has been tapped, he brings a reluctant Sarah along to protect her. A cryptic clue leads Frank and Sarah to an NYC Library, grandly portrayed by the Toronto Reference Library. As they ascend the glass elevator, the many levels that stretch out before them epitomize the sheer magnitude of their task, for they do not know what the proverbial needle in a haystack looks like. The largest public library in Canada is located at Yonge and Bloor, one of Toronto's busiest and most expensive intersections, and home to one of the world's largest Sherlock Holmes collections. The library is a building at odds with its environment and brimming with knowledge and mystery – much like Frank himself. It is a fitting place, not only to begin their quest, but also their romance. As the elevator rises, Frank casually demonstrates that he speaks Chinese. Sarah begins to realize that Frank too has many levels. In the library, they find a list of names which reveals the first piece of the puzzle and by the time it is solved, Sarah will discover why Frank is **R**etired, **E**xtremely **D**angerous.
⤷Fiona Luck

Directed by Robert Schwentke

Scene description: Retired agent Frank Moses and friend Sarah Ross uncover a clue as to why they are suddenly CIA targets

Timecode for scene: 0:26:53 – 0:29:09

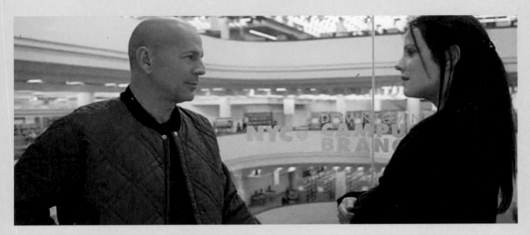

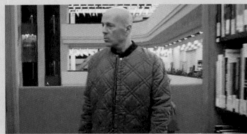

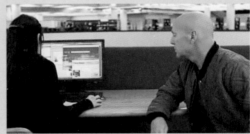

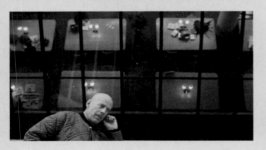

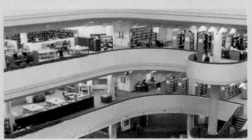

TAKE THIS WALTZ (2011)

Trinity Bellwoods Park

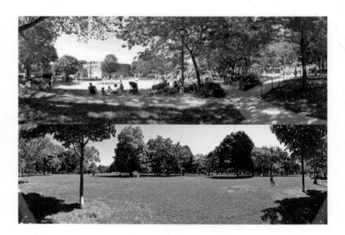

IT SEEMS it was not until relatively recently that Toronto had any worldly coolness to speak of but its recently gentrified west end gets a love letter in Sarah Polley's *Take This Waltz*. The emotionally naked film is set in the neighbourhood during a hot summer, full of torrid colours and amidst the new haunts of an emerging hipsturbia. Its characters inhabit neighbourhoods that, roughly a decade ago, were either declining industrial zones or just plain seedy. Today, the streets of West Queen West are lined by experimental restaurants and micro-breweries, and the revived neighbourhood's beating hipster heart is Trinity Bellwoods Park. Originally the site of the Anglican Trinity College, before it joined the University of Toronto a few kilometres to the east, the park has evolved from a dark patch of land across from the city's mental health hospital to the recreational hub for a growing community of urban condo dwellers. It is here that Daniel (Luke Kirby) and Margot (Michelle Williams) enjoy a picnic during a whirlwind tour of the city's cool spots, which also includes the nearby Lakeview restaurant and a significant ride on the Scrambler at the Centreville amusement park on Centre Island. *Take This Waltz* ultimately explores not only the ups and downs of its characters' relationships, but also, in a rare turn for cinematic Toronto, the sweltering, living city itself. ➦*David Fleischer*

Photos © Ontario Media Development Corporation

Directed by Sarah Polley
Scene description: The characters enjoy a day in the town, picnicking in Trinity Bellwoods Park
Timecode for scene: 1:12:12 – 1:13:00

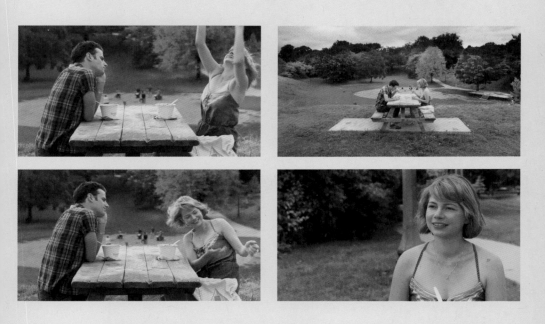

COSMOPOLIS (2012)

LOCATION *Union Station, 65 Front Street West*

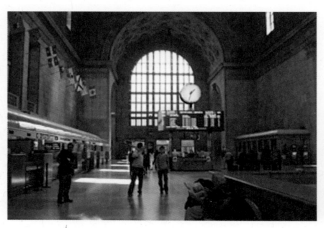
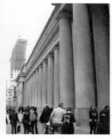

FILMED IN FRONT of Union Station, which serves as a terminal for some of Toronto's rail services, subway trains and buses, these establishing shots show a line of identical limousines parked one after another with their similarly attired drivers – factors that, as we shall see, likely contribute to Elise Shifrin's (Sarah Gadon) inability to locate her car. Director and adaptor David Cronenberg further ironizes his protagonist Eric Packer's (Robert Pattinson) and his peers' obsession with demonstrating their wealth and spending power in a subsequent scene, when his chief of finance (Emily Hampshire) wonders, 'What's the charm of identical?' He replies: 'That I'm a powerful person who chooses not to demarcate his territory with singular driblets of piss is what? Something I need to apologize for?' However, the symbols that Packer and his peers select for their self-representation are strikingly similar and they show only the characters' assimilation. The early and very rhythmic bars of composer Howard Shore's and the rock band Metric's score, the metallic columns that line the front of the limousine, the progression of cars, and the pillars of Union Station collectively foreshadow and replicate Packer's preoccupation with order, and it is unsurprising that he is worried when he learns of his asymmetrical prostate. As the film progresses, this obsession with geometry is repeatedly called into question: the stock market is shown as unpredictable, and Packer, despite battling traffic for the entire day, only had one side of his hair cut. **↦Tom Ue**

Photos © Tom Ue

Directed by David Cronenberg
Scene description: *Limousines are lined up in front of the Union Station in the film's establishing shots*
Timecode for scene: *0:01:14 – 0:02:27*

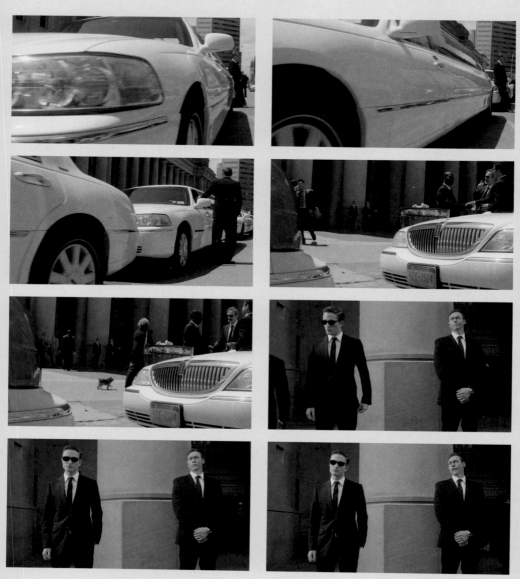

Images © 2012 Alfama Films/Prospero Pictures/Kinology

TOTAL RECALL (2012)

LOCATION

Lower Bay Subway Station at 64 Bloor Street West

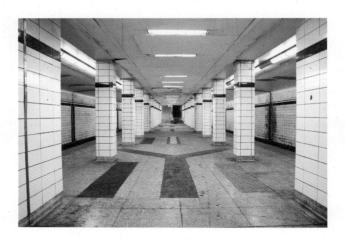

SET IN 2084, *Total Recall*'s Earth has only two livable territories that are overpopulated and wracked with dissent. Douglas Quaid (Colin Farrell) learns that hidden in his head is the key to stopping a robotic invasion. He and his lover Melina (Jessica Biel) are seeking the resistance leader Matthias (Bill Nighy) who can help unlock the answer. The pair absconds through a dilapidated subway station, a site that epitomizes the planet's bleakness, and onto a train that takes them out into the uninhabitable wasteland where they will find him. Despite the simplicity of Toronto's subway-line system, the Lower Bay Station was built in 1966 and was only used as a hub for six months. Repeated delays provoked the Toronto Transit Commission to make the system into two permanent lines. The station, while unused, has remained fully operational. It is utilized for crew and security training, moving vehicles from one line to another and, of course, film and television. Since the 1970s, Lower Bay has been the backdrop for dozens of films, so much so that they store a standing set of signs for other cities. While many Torontonians know about their 'secret' abandoned station, few have seen it, though they continue to claim that it is haunted by a woman in a red dress. *Total Recall* offers a romanticized notion of what they imagine it looks like: a neglected and forgotten derelict. In reality it is practical, reliable and, since there's no stunt train, the odds are good that you and Colin Farrell have shared a seat. ⟿*Fiona Luck*

Photo © Kevin Harrison

Directed by Len Wiseman
**Scene description: Douglas Quaid and Melina take a train
into the wastelands to search for rebel leader Matthias
Timecode for scene: 1:11:35 – 1:14:35**

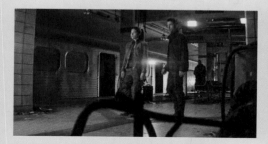 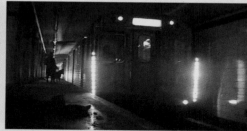

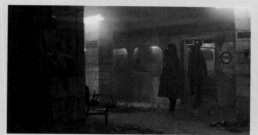 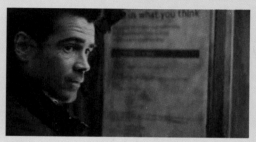

STORIES WE TELL (2012)

Wallace Avenue Footbridge

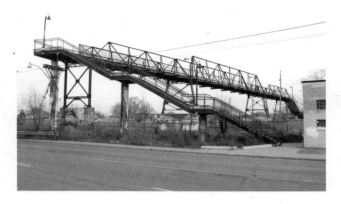

SARAH POLLEY'S *Stories We Tell* opens with a quote from Margaret Atwood's *Alias Grace* (1996), a novel which, like her film, is preoccupied with truths, witnessing and uncertainty. Polley explores her mother's life and, through piecing together conflicting accounts of it, investigates the story of her birth. It does so through bringing together interviews, written accounts by family members, and, as here, Super-8 footage recreations shot to look like home movies. In this sequence, Polley's mother Diane is happy and standing on Wallace Avenue Footbridge. The challenges of trying to determine if this is archival footage or a Super-8 recreation with Rebecca Jenkins playing Diane closely mirror and foreground those of telling a family story, which, as *Stories We Tell* reveals, is constantly shaped by the narrator, his or her personal feelings and the distortion of memory. Furthermore, the juxtaposition of this scene with other narratives from different periods, and the use, as an intertext, of Atwood's novel about one of the most notorious murders in Canadian history, all speak to the nature of the film and, indeed, life stories, as works of bricolage, realizing Atwood's quote about stories becoming what they are through narration. Sometimes, as *Stories We Tell* shows us, they take on lives of their own. **⟿Tom Ue**

Photo © Kevin Harrison

Directed by Sarah Polley
Scene description: *Footage of a scene with Sarah Polley's mother*
Timecode for scene: 0:00:26 – 0:00:30

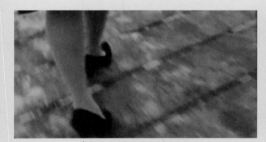 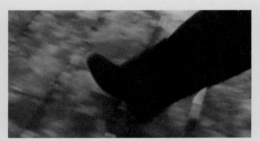

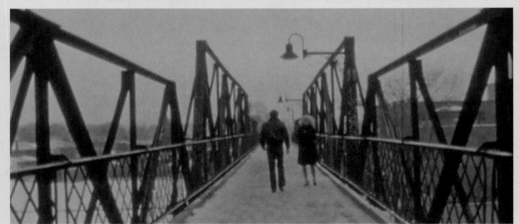

PACIFIC RIM (2013)

LOCATION *Hearn Generating Station, 440 Unwin Avenue*

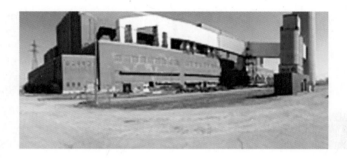

THE REPURPOSING OF abandoned industrial spaces for shooting is a longstanding tradition for films, ranging from abandoned power stations used by Terry Gilliam in *Brazil* (1985) and *Twelve Monkeys* (1995) to the old gasworks that Stanley Kubrick transformed into the Vietnamese city of Hue in the final act of *Full Metal Jacket* (1987). When Guillermo del Toro filmed *Pacific Rim* in Toronto, it was the biggest film production that the city had seen, even if it rarely ventured beyond computer-augmented soundstages. In a key scene, Stacker Pentecost (Idris Elba) heads up to Alaska to recruit the reluctant Raleigh Becket (Charlie Hunnam) to help battle the great monsters threatening humankind. Becket is working on a coastal wall at a perfectly cinematic industrial site filled with sweaty workers and flying sparks. This time, however, the construction is not a computer-generated construction but an actual piece of Toronto. From 1951 to 1991, the Hearn Generating Station provided power to the city. Today, the plant, located on Unwin Street in Toronto's Port Lands area, is quiet except for when Hollywood comes knocking. In the years since it closed, the Hearn has served as a prominent setting in *RED* (Robert Schwentke, 2010) and *Resident Evil: Retribution* (Paul W. S. Anderson, 2012) amongst others. In the two decades since it shut down, redevelopment plans have included a more modern power station, a film studio (of course) or even a series of hockey rinks, but for the time being it sits abandoned, its smokestack towering over the industrial Toronto that once was. ⇝ **David Fleischer**

Photo © Ontario Media Development Corporation

Scene description: Stacker Pentecost tries to convince Jaeger pilot
Raleigh Becket to return and help them fight the kaiju monsters
Timecode for scene: 0:21:00 – 0:23:01

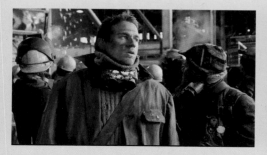 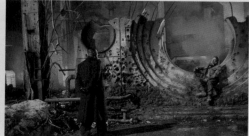

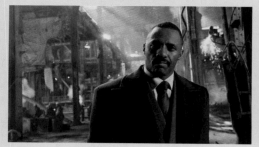 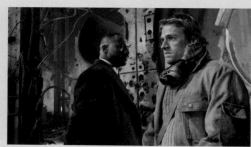

THE TORONTO INTERNATIONAL FILM FESTIVAL (TIFF) AND THE CITY

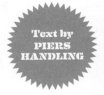

Text by
PIERS
HANDLING

Behind the scenes of TIFF's film selection

Our programming team (composed of eighteen programmers, including myself), travel around the world throughout the year in search of the best films to bring back to Toronto. Our team is on the road in one way or another – sitting on juries, attending other festivals from about October onwards. When we move into the New Year in January, the festivals start in a serious way with Sundance, followed by Berlin in February and Cannes in May. These festivals are very useful as networking opportunities, but we all do a lot of non-festival travel to see films, travelling to cities all over the world screening films and keeping in touch with our contacts. The team's extensive knowledge, wealth of expertise and unwavering commitment and passion for cinema guides the selection process to find the best films in the world. We all have a variety of industry contacts that we cultivate – film-makers, producers, distributors, sales agents, talent agencies – and this network provides us with most of the films we screen over the course of the year. Each programmer is given a certain number of programming slots and after that they are on their own, with complete freedom

to invite what they think is important. It is very competitive to get a film into Toronto with about a 10 per cent success ratio of films invited to films seen.

Most of the organization's departments start preparing for the festival around March and work in full swing throughout the summer leading up to the festival in early September. Our marketing and creative teams start rolling out promotional materials and ad campaigns, the Sales and Industry Office spearheads leading-edge industry initiatives, and the Communications Department begins accrediting media from around the globe over the summer but the planning is now year-round.

Once July comes around, we are in the thick of it – completely immersed in the final stages of the arduous selecting process: viewing and inviting films and film-makers. During this time we also work on the eleven-day schedule, wrap up meetings with movie studios and distributors, and start to host press conferences and issue press releases in late-July and continue steadily throughout the month of August.

TIFF's tradition of celebrating both Canadian and international cinema

We obviously have a special commitment to celebrating Canadian cinema but we are a relatively small film-producing country so clearly we also need to showcase the riches of world cinema. The heart of TIFF's mandate is to champion the creation of cinema from all parts of the world, reflecting diverse and differing perspectives and artistic viewpoints. Our permanent home, TIFF Bell Lightbox, has allowed us to continue this commitment. Our screenings, lectures, discussions, festivals and workshops, offer audiences the unique opportunity to delve into the deep riches of cinema history and culture. It is of vital importance for us to promote and nurture historical and contemporary Canadian cinema side by side with international cinema, and we do this both during the eleven-day festival in September

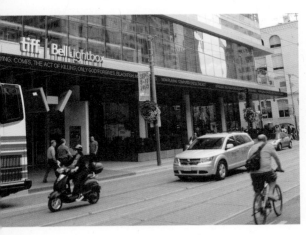

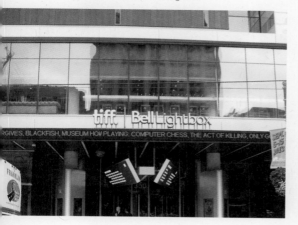

and year-round through our programming and industry initiatives at TIFF Bell Lightbox. By doing so, we not only showcase Canadian film to Canadians and to the world, but we are also providing a vital context and framework to watch and discuss Canadian cinema within the history of cinema; we are protecting our rich film heritage and championing the critical importance of film as an art form. We have a number of mentoring programmes for Canadian film-makers: Talent Lab, Rising Stars and Studio, and these are designed to provide our film-makers with unique professional opportunities.

September 2010 celebrated the opening of TIFF's new home, the TIFF Bell Lightbox

TIFF Bell Lightbox is located at the centre of the entertainment district in downtown Toronto. Occupying one city block, the combined space of the building encompasses over 153,000 square feet of multi-use space and includes over 1,300 cinema seats. It includes a three-storey atrium, five state-of-the-art cinemas, two galleries, three learning studios, our TIFF shop, TIFF's year-round box office, TIFF's Film Reference Library, staff offices, two concept restaurants by Oliver & Bonacini (O&B Canteen and Luma) and Malaparte, an event space on the sixth floor.

TIFF Bell Lightbox has enabled us to bring our diverse and unique range of existing programmes as well as new initiatives and community and industry events under one roof. With a permanent home we are now able to present the best of classic and contemporary.

How TIFF copes with developments in technology

While it is true that technology continues to develop and change by the minute and that it indeed has influenced the way films are made and shown around the world, we've found that audiences still cherish the experience of watching films on the big-screen in a communal and social setting. Having a state-of-the-art facility like ours gives us the capability to project a comprehensive range of formats (16 mm, 35 mm, 70 mm, a variety of video projection and DCP) in our cinemas. In addition to this, our Film Programmes team works arduously season after season to secure screening copies that best represent films in their original theatrical screening format whenever possible, and available, and that exemplify picture and sound technology concurrent with the film-maker's intention. This means audiences not only get the unique opportunity to experience contemporary and classic films as they were meant to be seen, but also, thanks to the unique curatorial voice of our programmers, their viewing experience is embedded within a context. Film-maker retrospectives, for example, invite film lovers to immerse themselves in the body of work of a director while national spotlights and genre specific programmes, inspire them to reflect on the connections between a group of films throughout a certain time or era.

As part of our commitment to enrich the movie-going experience, we also provide our audiences with exciting opportunities to engage directly with film-makers, actors, scholars and film professionals through Q&As, on-stage in-depth conversations, lectures and master classes. Some of the guests we've welcomed over the past three years have included John Waters, Isabella Rossellini, Woody Harrelson, Paul Haggis, Susan Sarandon, Geena Davis, Guillermo del Toro, Gena Rowlands, Anil Kapoor, Stevie Nicks, Jackie Chan, Johnnie To, David Cronenberg, Leos Carax and Ivan and Jason Reitman.

Indeed, I think the availability of 'films' on many platforms has resulted in a more-informed and educated audience who want to explore their passions in a deeper way – and that is why we built TIFF Bell Lightbox! People will always want to get together, to socialize and be around other people, and they are brought together by concerts, plays, and of course, films. ✦

GO FURTHER

Recommended reading, useful websites and film availability

BOOKS

Alias Grace
by Margaret Atwood
(Seal Books, 2000)

'By Way of an Introduction'
by Piers Handling
In Geoff Pevere et al. (eds), *Toronto on Film*
(TIFF, 2009) pp. 1–17

Unplanned Suburbs:
Toronto's American Tragedy, 1900 to 1950
by Richard Harris
(Johns Hopkins University Press, 1996)

Splitting Images:
Contemporary Canadian Ironies
by Linda Hutcheon
(Oxford University Press, 1991)

The Medium is the Massage:
An Inventory of Effects
by Marshall McLuhan and Quentin Fiore
(Bantam Books, 1967)

JOURNAL ARTICLES

'Film Festivals, Programming,
and the Building of a National Cinema'
by Liz Czach
In *The Moving Image* 4: 1 (2004) pp. 76–88

'No Nation but Adaptation: "The Bear
Came over the Mountain," Away from Her,
and What It Means to Be Faithful'
by Robert McGill
In *Canadian Literature*
197 (2008) pp. 98–111

FILM/TELEVISION

'The Bart Wants What It Wants'
Michael Polcino, dir.
In *The Simpsons*
Matt Groening, creator (Fox, 2002)

Ginger Snaps
John Fawcett, dir.
(TVA International, 2001)

ONLINE

Canadian Film Encyclopedia
http://tiff.net/canadianfilmencyclopedia

'College and Lansdowne/Then and Now'
http://losttoronto2.wordpresscom

Film, Television, Commercial and
Music Video Production Toronto 2012
– Year in Review
http://www.toronto.ca/

'History of the Distillery District' (n.d.)
http://www.thedistillerydistrict.com/history.php

'Reel Toronto'
http://torontoist.com/tag/reel-toronto

'Scott Pilgrim vs. The World:
Pilgrim's progress'
http://www.thestar.com/

CONTRIBUTORS

Editor and contributing writer biographies

EDITOR

TOM UE is Social Sciences and Humanities Research Council of Canada Doctoral Fellow and Canadian Centennial Scholar in the Department of English Language and Literature at University College London, where he researches Shakespeare's influence on the writing of Henry James, George Gissing and Oscar Wilde.

CONTRIBUTORS

COREY WAITE ARNOLD lives in Philadelphia, Pennsylvania where he is pursuing an MA in English at Villanova University. He specializes in post-1945 and contemporary American literature, with a focus on trauma studies and the emerging canon of 9/11 literature and film.

NOEL BROWN received his PhD in Film from Newcastle University in 2010, where he has taught courses on film and literature. Currently an independent scholar, his primary research interests are in classical and modern Hollywood cinema, particularly the historical dimensions of the family film; children's film and television globally; contemporary youth cultures; and genre film.

SHERI CHRIQUI is a PhD candidate in Medieval English at Royal Holloway, University of London. Sheri earned an M.Phil. in Medieval English at the University of Oxford and an MA in English at Clark University. Her work focuses on medieval romance, Arthurian literature, manuscript studies, heraldry, and myth-making.

MICHAEL DA SILVA is a student in the University of Toronto Faculty of Law's Doctor of Juridical Science Program. His undergraduate studies at Dalhousie University included a Minor in Film Studies.

RICHARD DENNIS teaches historical and cultural geography at University College London. His research focuses on nineteenth- and early twentieth-century cities in Britain and North America.

LAI-TZE FAN is a PhD candidate in the York and Ryerson Joint Graduate Program in Communication and Culture. Her research examines the influence of digital epistemologies and poetics in contemporary print literature.

DAVID FLEISCHER is a Toronto-based writer who graduated from the University of Toronto shortly after the filming of *Good Will Hunting* (Gus van Sant, 1997). He has covered everything from urban issues to arts and entertainment and his articles have appeared in publications including the *National Post* and *The Globe and Mail*.

STEVE GRAVESTOCK has worked for the Toronto International Film Festival since 1995, and he began programming for the festival in 1997. Gravestock has contributed to the Canadian feature film selection process since 2004, and he also selects films from Scandinavia, the Philippines and the Netherlands; previously, he programmed films from India and Australia.

PIERS HANDLING is Director and Chief Executive Officer of TIFF. He has held this position since 1994, and is responsible for leading both the operational and artistic growth of the organization. Under Handling's direction, the organization has grown to become an internationally renowned cultural institution.

JOHN JAMES is the author of poetry and criticism, which has appeared in *Boston Review*, *The Kenyon Review*, *Hayden's Ferry Review*, *Washington Square*, *Pleiades*, and elsewhere.

FIONA LUCK is an eclectic mix of spirit, blood and character. Born in Glasgow and raised partly in the Scottish highlands and partly in suburban Canada, her Scottish, English, Chinese and Guyanese family made her a natural at living in multicultural Toronto. Luck has taught English, history and a range of courses in the arts, humanities and social sciences from Grades 7 to the now extinct 13.

GEORGIA RUSHING MACEY is a writer, editor and film-maker in Los Angeles, California. She studied English at Delta State University in Cleveland, Mississippi, and at Clark University in Worcester, Massachusetts, where she focused primarily on Shakespeare in text and performance. In the last year, she has produced, directed, shot and edited over 25 short films, as well as working as the casting director for an episodic Western.

ROBERT MCGILL is a writer and professor of English at the University of Toronto. He has published two novels, *The Mysteries* (McClelland & Stewart, 2004) and *Once We Had a Country* (Knopf Canada, 2013), as well as a non-fiction book, *The Treacherous Imagination: Intimacy, Ethics, and Autobiographical Fiction* (Ohio State University Press, 2013).

TYLER SHORES is a writer and independent scholar with research interests in literature and digital technology, history of reading and book culture. He has given talks on digital culture and literature, philosophy, and popular culture, and he has worked as a director for non-profit book publishing, and at Google as part of Authors@Google, one of the world's most successful online lecture series.

WILL STRAW is Professor of Art History and Communications Studies at McGill University in Montreal and Director of the McGill Institute for the Study of Canada. He is the co-editor of the Canadian Cinema series (University of Toronto Press) and the author of over 120 articles on film, media and popular culture.

CARL WILSON is an associate lecturer in media at Sheffield College. He writes on a variety of topics, including Hitchcock, Welles, video games, expressionism, Charlie Kaufman, gangsters, reflexivity, sport films, screenwriting, thrillers, indie films, comic books and Jackie Chan.

FILMOGRAPHY

All films mentioned or featured in this book

8 Mile (2002)	24
A Christmas Story (1983)	5,11,20
A Dangerous Method (2001)	88
A History of Violence (2005)	91,96
American Psycho (2000)	43,54
Ararat (2002)	75,78
Assault on Precinct 13 (2005)	91,92
Avengers, The (2012)	106
Away From Her (2006)	7,126,129
Billy Madison (1995)	27,36
Black Stallion, The (1979)	41
Blue Velvet (1986)	89
Blues Brothers, The (1980)	52
Blues Brothers 2000 (1998)	43,52,89
Bowling For Columbine (2002)	75,80
Boy Meets Girl (1998)	57
Brazil (1985)	122
Chicago (2002)	7,41,75,82
Chloe (2009)	91,104
Cinderella Man (2005)	4,91,94
Cleopatra (1963)	6
Cocktail (1988)	27,32
Cosmopolis (2012)	1,5,7,88,109,116
Crash (1996)	43,46,88,89
Crash (2004)	46
Dead Ringers (1988)	89
Death to Smoochy (2002)	59,70
Drying Up the Streets (1978)	24,25
Eastern Promises (2007)	88
Enemy (2013)	2
F Word, The (2013)	2,6
Fever Pitch (2005)	50
Five Senses, The (1999)	57
Fly, The (1986)	88
Flowers On a One Way Street (1967)	24
Frequency (2000)	41,59,62,92
Full Metal Jacket (1987)	122
Ginger Snaps (2000)	59,66
Goin' Down the Road (1970)	24
Good Will Hunting (1997)	6,43,50,128
Great Toronto Fire,The (1904)	6
Hairspray (2007)	5,91,98
Highpoint (1982)	11,16
Hulk (2003)	100
Incredible Hulk, The (2008)	91,100,106
I've Heard the Mermaids Singing (1987)	56,57
Jay and Silent Bob Strike Back (2001)	50
Johnny Mnemonic (1995)	27,38
Kick-Ass (2010)	106,107
Kick-Ass 2 (2013)	107

Kids in the Hall: Brain Candy (1996)	41
Killing Fields, The (1984)	27,28
L.A. Confidential (1997)	25
Love Guru, The (2008)	44,89
Maximum Risk (1996)	41,43,44
My Big Fat Greek Wedding (2002)	75,76
Nobody Waved Goodbye (1964)	5,6,8,9,24
Next of Kin (1984)	56,57
Offering, The (1967)	9
Only Thing You Know, The (1971)	9,25
Pacific Rim (2013)	2,109,122
Paddle to the Sea (1966)	11,12
Perfectly Normal (1991)	27,34,73
Peyton Place (1957)	89
Police Academy (1984)	11,22
Pompeii (2014)	7
Prince and Me, The (2004)	75,84
Princess Bride, The (1987)	6
Producers, The (1968)	24
Project Grizzly (1996)	56
Recruit, The (2003)	41
Red (2010)	109,112,122
Resident Evil: Apocalypse (2004)	75,86
Resident Evil: Retribution (2012)	122
Rio Bravo (1959)	92
Road Kill (1989)	57
Rumble in the Bronx (1995)	98
Scott Pilgrim vs the World (2010)	5,41,72,107,109,110,126
Shadows (1959)	9
Short Circuit 2 (1988)	27,30
Silent Partner, The (1978)	11,14,24,57,72
Skulls, The (2000)	59,60
Stories We Tell (2012)	109,120
Sweet Hereafter, The (1997)	43,48
Take This Waltz (2011)	72,109,114
This Movie is Broken (2010)	57
Three Men and a Baby (1987)	41
Three to Tango (1999)	41
Ticket to Heaven (1981)	24
Top of His Head (1989)	57
Toronto Stories (2008)	91,102
Total Recall (2012)	109,118
Trapped in Paradise (1994)	41
Twelve Monkeys (1995)	122
Videodrome (1983)	11,18,73,89
Wes Craven Presents: Dracula 2000 (2000)	59,68
Winter Kept Us Warm (1965)	8,9
X-Men (2000)	40,41,59,44,64,89
X-Men: First Class (2011)	41